WITHDRAWN

Knockout interview answers

D1393367

brilliantideas

one good idea can change your life...

Knockout interview answers

High-performance techniques to clinch your dream job

Ken Langdon and Nikki Cartwright

3WK
331.128 LAN
13,39
CAREERS

A37477

EALING TERTIARY COLLEGE
ACTON CENTRE LIBRARY

CAREFUL NOW

Unlike financial advisers, solicitors and psychiatrists, career and interview advisers have no regulatory body; so we have decided to put in our own disclaimer. If you follow all our advice, give the sample answers we suggest and work out where each of your interviewers is coming from using our experience, we think you'll probably get the job. But if you don't – hey we did our best. What probably happened is that some interviewer refused to act to type – and it's completely their fault – nothing to do with us. Nothing that we've said is wrong, nada, nix, not a sausage and it's not our fault – completely, totally, absolutely not our fault. *(That's enough disclaimers – Ed.)*

Copyright © The Infinite Ideas Company Limited, 2005

The rights of Ken Langdon and Nikki Cartwright to be identified as the authors of this book has been asserted in accordance with the Copyright, Designs and Patents Act 1988

First published in 2005 by
The Infinite Ideas Company Limited
36 St Giles
Oxford
OX1 3LD
United Kingdom
www.infideas.com

All rights reserved. Except for the quotation of small passages for the purposes of criticism and review, no part of this publication may be reproduced, stored in a retrieval system or transmitted in any form or by any means, electronic, mechanical, photocopying, recording, scanning or otherwise, except under the terms of the Copyright, Designs and Patents Act 1988 or under the terms of a licence issued by the Copyright Licensing Agency Ltd, 90 Tottenham Court Road, London W1T 4LP, UK, without the permission in writing of the publisher. Requests to the publisher should be addressed to the Permissions Department, Infinite Ideas Limited, 36 St Giles, Oxford OX1 3LD, UK or faxed to +44 (0)1865 514777.

A CIP catalogue record for this book is available from the British Library.

ISBN 1-904902-46-4

Brand and product names are trademarks or registered trademarks of their respective owners.

Designed and typeset by Baseline Arts Ltd, Oxford
Printed and bound by TJ International, Cornwall

A37477

Brilliant ideas

   Some interviewers are better than others. Good ones use open questions like this one to
   open you up and get you talking. Poorer ones fall into the trap of asking closed questions.
   Look out for open questions – you want them because they give you the chance to make
   your points.

   The HR people will probably interview you at some point. Even if they don't you can bet
   that they're talking to the other interviewers behind the scenes. Understanding what
   they're looking for gives you competitive edge.

   Delivering great answers to the interviewer's questions is the main skill in impressing
   people and getting the job; but let's not underestimate the importance of the body
   language you use to get your nose in front.

   Prepare for this one by thinking about yourself from other people's perspectives. Make
   sure you use examples to show, firstly, that you do know how people see you and,
   secondly, that you learn from their feedback.

Brilliant features

Each chapter of this book is designed to provide you with an inspirational idea that you can read quickly and put into practice straight away.

Throughout you'll find four features that will help you to get right to the heart of the idea:

- *Here's an idea for you* Take it on board and give it a go – right here, right now. Get an idea of how well you're doing so far.

- If this idea looks like a life-changer then there's no time to lose. *Try another idea* will point you straight to a related tip to enhance and expand on the first.

- *Defining ideas* Words of wisdom from masters and mistresses of the art, plus some interesting hangers-on.

- *How did it go?* If at first you do succeed, try to hide your amazement. If, on the other hand, you don't, this is where you'll find a Q and A that highlights common problems and how to get over them.

Introduction

So you've found the right job opportunity, you've sent in your immaculately prepared CV: all that's left to land the working life of your dreams is to win at the interview. The art of successful interviews includes the art of interesting and free-flowing conversation. It's also about technique – techniques for interviewing and techniques for being interviewed. Here's how to bone up on great answers to the interviewers' questions, and to make sure you understand exactly what they're looking for.

Despite scientific advances in hiring techniques such as assessment centres and psychometric testing (if you don't know now, you'll know what they are when you've read the relevant chapters), the interview remains the main way that managers decide which people they invite to work for them. It's an interesting struggle, the one between interviewee and interviewer, in that both sides can win. The hiring company can get the right person and the candidate can get a job that they are right for and that is right for them.

But it's competitive, of course. In most interview situations there are other people bidding for the same job. Beating them off means thinking about and rehearsing good answers to the most popular questions that'll be thrown at you. This book covers all the standard questions you're likely to be asked, (on pages 232–5 you'll find an index of all the questions covered) and suggests prize-winning answers. And then it does a bit more.

There's an ancient Chinese saying, 'Give a person a fish and they eat for a day; give a person a fishing rod and they eat for the rest of their lives.' The fish are the answers to the questions you'll find in the chapters; the fishing rod is the explanation of where the interviewer is coming from and what they're looking for. After all, most of the people who are going to interview you have had some training in interview techniques. Some of them, the human resources (HR) people, have spent a lot of their working lives studying how to prepare for and use the interview to get the right person for the job.

So, it's taken a combination of two people with different backgrounds to come up with the answer to the interview question. Ken has a lot of experience in conducting interviews from a line manager's perspective. He's also spent a lot of time influencing people in interview situations as a salesman, account manager and sales manager. Nikki has learnt and developed the theory as well as the practice of interviewing in her capacity as an HR director.

We'll talk about being scrupulously honest; but we'll also show you how to give that honesty the best possible spin. We'll look at exploiting your strengths and putting your weaknesses into a context where not only do they not matter but by the end of the interview may very well have metamorphosed into strengths. After all, though everyone wants a win/win result, the point of going to an interview is to be offered the job. So, yes, you need to be open so that they see the real you; but, yes, you need a bit of guile as well to put you out in front as the candidate with what it really takes.

If you do all this preparation you might be wondering if it's all right to take a folder in with you containing your notes. That's fine. But be careful: they don't like it if it looks as though you're reading a prepared script; so keep the notes brief, just reminders of the stories and examples you're going to use to plead your case.

ACKNOWLEDGEMENTS

Our thanks to David, Katherine, Rebecca and Richard, the publishers, whose patience Ken severely tested. Our thanks also to Sally Ariff and Alan Bonham, who gave us some excellent ideas.

Nikki would like to dedicate this book to her adorable parents with love and gratitude for being such brilliant role models.

What interests you about our particular industry?

Some interviewers are better than others. Good ones use open questions like this one to open you up and get you talking. Poorer ones fall into the trap of asking closed questions. Look out for open questions – you want them because they give you the chance to make your points.

Recognising an open question helps you to understand how in principle you're going to give them answers that knock their socks off and it can even help you to give a good answer to a bad question.

Overheard at a sales training course:

Rookie salesperson: *'I'm not quite getting this. Could you just give me an example of an open question?'*

Trainer: *'Why?'*

Rookie salesperson: *'Because maybe I'll understand an example better than I understand the theory.'*

Trainer:	*'Why?'*
Rookie salesperson:	*'Oh, this is getting so frustrating! Why don't you just give me an example?'*
Trainer:	*'Ah, now that's a good question.'*

Here is the single-word open question 'Why' doing its job beautifully. Although the rookie doesn't yet understand what an open question is, she does exactly what the questioner wants. She makes the person answering give honest and instinctive answers.

Here's an idea for you...

Have a conversation with some colleagues or friends in which you only ask open questions. Try to do as little of the talking as you possibly can. Ask them questions about themselves, their families, their interests and so on. You'll be surprised how easy it is to get them talking and opening up about themselves. There are two benefits to doing this exercise. One is that you will appreciate what a skilled interviewer is trying to do and the second is that it makes you listen, another great interview skill.

DISPLAYING KNOWLEDGE IN ANSWERING OPEN QUESTIONS

'What interests you about our industry?' is an open question. It requires you to reveal what you know about the business the organisation is in and why you are interested in being involved in it. So be prepared. A poor answer to this question, particularly one that demonstrates that you don't know anything about the industry or the organisation, is a showstopper that'll get you off to the poorest possible start. In fact, many people regard it as quite rude for an interviewee not to have done such basic research.

Good interviewers use a 'funnel' technique in their questioning. They start with a very open question and then funnel down deeper and deeper into specifics. So, it's always dangerous to say anything that you can't substantiate or expand on.

It's easy enough nowadays to brief yourself on an industry using the internet. Look not only at the website of the organisation you're thinking of joining but also at their main competitors. Look for how fast the industry is growing, how profitable it is and how much change has occurred in recent years. All of these investigations lead you to a good answer. You can be interested in the business no matter what state it is in. 'I want to take part in the rapid growth and change that is taking place in the telecommunications industry. I'm excited about being involved in a rapidly changing market where you have to be very light on your feet to keep up with the competition.' Or alternatively, 'The food-retailing industry is very interesting because over many years you've developed very detailed and sophisticated answers to all the tough business problems such as branding, planned discounting and so on. I think I can learn most and quickest in such an environment.'

If possible, tie your interest in the industry into an interest you've had from an early age. You will see further relevance of this in IDEA 46, *Would it be OK for you to go and see our occupational psychologist?*

Try another idea...

'I keep six honest serving men (They taught me all I knew) Their names are What and Why and When And How and Where and Who'
RUDYARD KIPLING

Defining idea...

Another good source of information is the company's annual report. Have a look at the mission statement and try to find out why you want to be involved with an organisation with this particular stated aim. Quote from a recent newspaper article to show that you're taking an interest. (If it's a big organisation then go into any newspaper site and search for the name of the company. If it's smaller then use a search engine and you'll probably come up with something.)

USING WELL-PREPARED ANSWERS

The industry sector will come up in some way whether they ask the question this way or not; so it's good technique to have the actual words you're going to use in your head before you go in. In fact all the preparation you've done in this area will help at some point in the interview. It just shows that you're keen to be part of the business that, after all, the interviewer is giving a large chunk of their working life to.

Now think about the question as asked by a less skilled interviewer: 'Are you interested in our industry?' This is an easy closed question – as if you're going to say, 'No, I'd much rather be in showbiz'! Answer it as though it were an open one. In fact it's the same answer with a slightly different starting point.

Q   **I tried this at a recent interview where I didn't win: I used some knowledge of their industry, including the phrase 'strategic partnerships', a term I got from their annual report. He came back asking what I meant by the term and I tried to explain but plainly looked out of my depth. That's the danger of this technique, isn't it: they'll see through your scant knowledge?**

A   *Try not to bluff them in an area where they obviously know tons more than you. Think about possible follow-up questions and then when you use a bit of their jargon finish by asking them what they mean by the term. 'I see your strategy revolves around "strategic partnerships". Can you tell me what that phrase means in this particular organisation?'*

Q   **In an interview I just went to I asked the interviewer some open questions. She then went on for about ten minutes without asking me a question. That doesn't give me a chance to convey to her how I'm right for the job, does it?**

A   *Possibly not, but in the grand majority of cases people most enjoy conversations if they've done most of the talking. Relax and let them talk themselves into hiring you.*

How did it go?

5

T

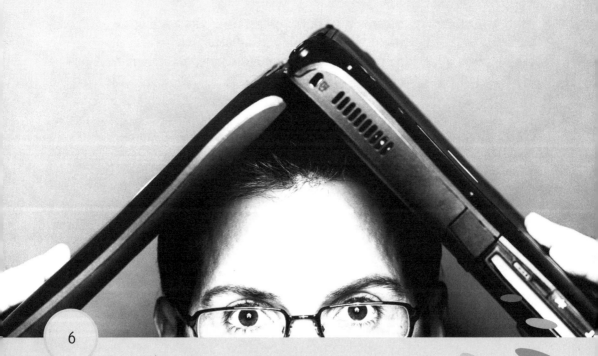

2

What makes you a good leader?

The HR people will probably interview you at some point. Even if they don't you can bet that they're talking to the other interviewers behind the scenes. Understanding what they're looking for gives you competitive edge.

Human resources managers have got 'degrees in people' and they're looking for talent, not just someone to do this job. They want people who'll do this job well and have potential for the future.

You can pretty much sum up the HR, or 'personnel', interest at an interview in terms of leadership skills. They want to know how you will shape up if you're given the tricky job of leading a team in their organisation. So before we look at good answers to this question let's agree on what they're probing for and, not least, what leadership is. Let's start from what it's not:

Team member to non-leader:	'Sorry to trouble you but I've got a bit of a problem at home. My mother-in-law is staying with us and she's starting to make life impossible for my wife.'
Non-leader:	'That's not a problem, mate. My wife wants a divorce; now that's a problem!'

The old cliché is true: the best communicators are listeners. Leaders always concentrate on the interests of their people. In fact a good leader may very well know a lot more about you than you do about them.

THIS QUESTION IS ABSOLUTELY ABOUT YOU

Leadership capabilities are the attributes that make you successful, your personal attributes if you like, or what you are naturally good at. Human resources managers are looking at your character as well as your innate ability to manage people and influence how they go about their jobs. Leadership's also to do with energy and getting things done. Many organisations asking a question in this area are also probing for the values that a person brings to the workplace. Everyone needs leadership skills and drive, whether they manage people or not. They're trying to answer the question, 'Can this person achieve success by influencing other people inside and outside the organisation?'

Here's an idea for you...

Have a look at your last appraisal. Is there anything there you can use as proof that someone else has noted your natural abilities in the leadership area? It's always more powerful to quote someone else than point out, modestly of course, how brilliant you think you are.

So plan your answer to include a number of these attributes and try to prove them by evidence or example as well as simple assertion. A safe place to start is two of the key attributes of a natural leader – resilience and flexibility. 'I find that I am generally the first person in my team to recover after a setback and generate the idea that starts to get us back on track.' This is a good double-pronged answer showing resilience and your ability to create new ideas. 'A good manager I worked for once demonstrated to me how important it is to be flexible in how you handle people. She treated everyone as unique individuals and got the best out of us in quite different ways.'

IDEA 17, *What is the one thing your team would most like to change about you?* gives further clues on leading people, listening to them and responding to their needs.

Try another idea...

Your 'values' as a leader are a touch more tricky. You'll probably demonstrate your values as you go through the interview, but if you want to use an open question like this to make the point, the safest way is to link it to the research you did on the organisation. 'On your website you talk about "quality driving everything we do" and that attracted me. I've always been competitive and I like to do things properly.' Be careful with this one, though; don't lay it on with a trowel. 'Values' is an area where the candidate can be a bit soupy or insincere. The key is to interpret particular values and make sense of them within your job.

TRUST ME, I'M A LEADER

Perhaps the most difficult element of this question is the assertion that people can trust you. You can only do this by example. Try telling them what you did to gain the trust of the team you're working with currently. Or do it the harder way of talking about behaviour from a member of your team which you regarded as inappropriate; what did you say and do about it? This is another double-pronged answer because it demonstrates that the organisation can trust you and the values you work within.

'The final test of leaders is that they leave behind them in other people the conviction and the will to carry on.'
WALTER LIPPMANN, US journalist

Defining idea...

9

How did it go?

Q **I'm going for an internal promotion and I really know what you mean about 'values' and people being mawkish about them. Top management has just produced a new version of our values and everyone is mouthing off about them in a way that I can't do because it sounds like so much management-speak. I'll have to talk about them, though, because they are very much flavour of the month. Do you think that's all right?**

A *Try saying just that to them: 'I have a slight concern that people are learning the words of the new values but not necessarily demonstrating them. This makes me a bit uncomfortable.' This could lead to a good discussion. Keep an eye on the HR person's reactions when you try this, though.*

Q **They asked me to tell them about a time when I had ignored company procedures because I felt that they were impeding my ability to complete a project. I thought it was a trick question and told them that I felt the procedures were there for a purpose and would not normally have such an effect. My instincts immediately told me that this wasn't a good answer. Were they right?**

A *Yes, 'fraid so. Organisations expect leaders to take risks with their career as well as with the company's resources. You need to show how you thought through the dilemma and made a good judgement. Good leaders will let company policy go hang if it's stopping them achieving their objectives.*

3

Please, take a seat

Delivering great answers to the interviewer's questions is the main skill in impressing people and getting the job; but let's not underestimate the importance of the body language you use to get your nose in front.

Neurolinguistic programming can help you to develop rapport very quickly in an interview.

It includes techniques that can help you at the beginning of the interview when you're getting over your nerves and the interviewers are forming their first impression.

MATCHING AND MIRRORING

Interviews are like speed dating. You quickly eye each other up and decide whether or not you're interested in taking things further. So you need to be able to build rapport with your interviewer as quickly and effectively as possible. You never have a second chance to make a first impression.

The key skill to use here is mirroring. Mirroring body language is based on the theory that we are more at ease, subconsciously, with people who are similar to ourselves. It's a bit like dancing. You can mirror most things:

Here's an idea for you...

It's probably best not to try the technique of mirroring for the first time in an interview. First of all, observe people doing it naturally at social gatherings. That gives you visual evidence that people do it, even in groups. Now try it in conversation with someone you know well, and then try it in a business context. Just a few practices should make you proficient enough to do it at an interview.

Posture, for instance. If they're upright, so are you. If they cross their legs, so do you. If their arms are on the table, so are yours. If you're sitting opposite someone with their right leg crossed, you cross your left leg to make a mirror image. You're making the person feel comfortable that they're talking to someone with similar behaviours to theirs.

Listen to the tone and speed of their voice. If they talk quickly, try to answer at the same speed. Vary your tone in the same way they do. Is the language they use concise or detailed? If they ask long questions they're going to be more comfortable with you giving a detailed answer.

Pick up on their mood, whether it's humorous or serious. You will notice, of course, how formally or casually they dress and conduct themselves.

You can mirror their use of gestures to accentuate a point. If they change their posture, you change yours. (People who are brilliant at this technique claim to match the speed at which a person's eyes blink, but beginners shouldn't try this lest they look like a mole emerging into sunlight.)

Thanks for buying one of our books! If you'd like to be placed on our mailing list to receive more information on forthcoming releases in the **52 Brilliant Ideas** series just send an e-mail to *info@infideas.com* with your name and address or simply fill in the details below and pop this card in the post. No postage is needed. We promise we won't do silly things like bombard you with lots of junk mail, nor would we even consider letting third parties look at your details. Ever.

Name:...

Address:..

....

e-mail:..

Which book did you purchase?...................................

....

Tell us what you thought of this book and our series; check out the 'Brilliant Communication' bit on the other side of this card.

I am interested in the following subjects:

☐ Health & relationships
☐ Lifestyle & leisure
☐ Arts, literature and music

☐ Careers, finance & personal development
☐ Sports, hobbies & games
☐ Actually, I'd be quite interested in:..............................

And just to say thanks, every month we'll pick 3 random names from a hat (ok, it may be some other cylindrical device) and send a complimentary book from the series. It could be you. So please tell us what book you'd like:..(check out www.52brilliantideas.com for a full list of our titles, or if you prefer we can choose one for you based on your subject interest).

You can change your life with brilliant ideas.

We're passionate about the effect our books have and we have designed them so that they can become an inspiring part of your daily routine. Our books help people to grow, giving them the confidence to believe in themselves and to transform their lives. Every day, around the world, people are regaining control of their lives with our brilliant ideas.

infiniteideas

www.52brilliantideas.com

BY AIR MAIL
par avion

Royal Mail

IBRS/CCRI NUMBER:
PHQ-D/9423/OX

NE PAS AFFRANCHIR

NO STAMP REQUIRED

RESPONSE PAYEE
GRANDE-BRETAGNE

Infinite Ideas Ltd
36 St Giles
OXFORD
GREAT BRITAIN
OX1 3LD

BrilliantCommunication

- If you enjoyed this book and find yourself cuddling it at night, please tell us. If you think this book isn't fit to use as kindling, please let us know. We value your thoughts and need your honest feedback. We know if we listen to you we'll get it right. Why not send us an e-mail at *listeners@infideas.com*.

- Do you have a brilliant idea of your own that our author has missed? E-mail us at *yourauthor missedatrick@infideas.com* and if it makes it into print in a future edition or appears on our web site we'll send you four books of your choice OR the cash equivalent. You'll be fully credited (if you want) so that everyone knows you've had a brilliant idea.

- Finally, if you've enjoyed one of our books why not become an **Infinite Ideas Ambassador**. Simply e-mail ten of your friends enlightening them about the virtues of the **52 Brilliant Ideas** series and dishing out our web address: www.52brilliantideas.com. Make sure you copy us in at *ambassador@infideas.com*. We promise we won't contact them unless they contact us, but we'll send you a free book of your choice for every ten friends you email. Help spread the

Don't mimic them or copy their gestures too quickly. Mirroring is a subtle technique and interviewers who are not NLP proficient should not consciously notice what you're doing. They will just get the warm feeling that comes from dealing with someone on the same wavelength.

The importance of eye contact is discussed in IDEA 32, *May I pass you over now to my colleague?*

Try another idea...

We all use this form of body language when we're relaxed with our friends. Watch people in a restaurant or a pub and you'll see how mirroring helps the group to feel comfortable in each other's company. Or maybe it's the other way round: when you're with someone you're entirely comfortable with, it's quite hard not to do it.

ANCHORING

You're never at your most confident when you're about to try to be tested, professionally and personally. Anchoring can be very helpful in removing the signs of nervousness and helping to give you the confidence to give of your best. Anchor yourself to a memory of a time in your life when you felt really confident. Before the interview, perhaps outside the door, pause and bring that experience of total confidence into your mind. Hold it there, remember how you felt and what you saw and said. This reminds your brain of how to feel and look confident. At times of pressure in the interview, recall the situation again and you'll adjust your behaviour back to expressing confidence.

'She is the mirror of alle courteisye.'
GEOFFREY CHAUCER

Defining idea...

15

How did
it go?

Q   I was mirroring an HR person in an interview. After ten minutes he
made three quite quick changes in the position of his arms and
legs. I followed as slowly as I could. He then flung his arms back,
stuck his legs right out until he was almost lying on the chair. I
couldn't mirror this even if I'd wanted to, because I was wearing a
skirt. What was going on?

A   *We think he sussed you. Your movements were not subtle enough, or he
was expert in NLP and saw what you were doing. He was also probably
teasing you; I suppose everyone has to have their bit of fun and lots of HR
folk don't get out that much. You did right to abandon your deliberate
attempt to mirror his body language.*

Q   I get terribly stressed out about interviews and never do myself
justice. I tried anchoring and it worked quite well to begin with.
Halfway through the interview, someone else joined us and I
started to feel really nervous. I didn't have time to think about the
anchor again and the rest of the interview suffered as a result. Is
it really possible to bring a happy time back into your mind in such
circumstances?

A   *Yes. Most interviewers will understand if you want to pause for breath.
Generally, we're all too quick to reply to questions in this environment
anyway. Practise taking pauses when you're in conversation. Pauses make
you look thoughtful and pay an interviewer the compliment that their
question was good enough to cause you to think. In those pauses you can
recall your anchor. Try to control your breathing. If you get nervous you
tend to talk from your throat rather than your diaphragm. Deep breathing
will help with this and make you appear more confident.*

4

How does your present team see you?

Prepare for this one by thinking about yourself from other people's perspectives. Make sure you use examples to show, firstly, that you do know how people see you and, secondly, that you learn from their feedback.

Your prospective line manager may well use this sort of question to satisfy himself that you will fit into the team context he has planned for you.

Start with a positive point that you believe is a key strength in your ability to get the best out of people. It's wise too to make this point using an unusual answer that doesn't seem to come straight out of the management books. Maybe, 'Two members of the team have given me some interesting feedback. They thanked me for being very supportive of them inside our organisation. I think it's my job to understand how the organisation really works. This helps me to navigate internal politics and processes and so enable the team to get on with the work in an efficient and productive way.'

Here's an idea for you...

Preparation for this is quite straightforward. Make sure you have asked as many team members as you can what their perception of you is. If it is at all possible to tell them what you are doing, then do so. They will probably enjoy helping you to prepare for this question. Incidentally the more open your relationship with your team is the better will be their contribution to your preparation. Make sure they always feel able to talk to you and give you feedback.

STAY PEOPLE NOT PROCESS ORIENTED

It is probably best not to see this question as being about your management style. Nor is it appropriate to answer it with a short dissertation on objective- as opposed to task-based managers. Stay with your real impact on your people. The interviewers are looking for a high degree of self-insight here. 'Although I know it's my job to explain the organisation's strategy to my team, I also want them to be able to work without having to worry about that. They need to be able to rely on me to set objectives that reflect that strategy.'

Think about why good people want to work for you. 'They know I'm a net exporter of managers and team members to other parts of the organisation.' Most people want to work for a manager who will not stand in their way if there is an opportunity to make progress or to be promoted by moving jobs.

GOING WELL? TAKE A LITTLE RISK

If you feel that the interview is going well and that you have good rapport with the interviewer it's a good idea to show how you learn from either your mistakes or feedback from your team. (Much better to use feedback from your team as an example, rather than feedback from your boss.)

'I got quite a shock about eighteen months ago when a member of my team told me that I seemed to "glaze over" when she talked about her personal situation. She said that I wasn't unhelpful and indeed that I asked her some good questions and even made some suggestions if she asked for them. It was just that I looked as though I didn't want to be involved in that particular conversation. Since then I have made sure that when such a discussion starts my body language and eye contact make it clear that I am interested and want to help.'

The management style thing arises in IDEA 36, *What's your style of influencing people?*

Try another idea...

If you are at an internal interview the chances are that the interviewer will have talked to one or two members of your team. They will also have heard your peer team leaders discussing your strengths and weaknesses. So don't overstate any perception that you want your team to have of you if there's any chance that it might have been contradicted. Look for hints of this when supplementary questions come in such as, 'Do they think that you have enough influence in getting a senior manager to change something if it would help them?' Don't duck it; at least tell them you are working on that area of the team leader's job.

**'O wad some Power the gift to gie us
To see ourselves as others see us!
It wad frae many a blunder free us,
And foolish notion.'**
ROBERT BURNS

Defining idea...

How did
it go?

Q **The annual appraisal system in my organisation includes a section on how my people see me and so on. That's enough, isn't it? Surely we don't want to encourage people to give their opinions all the time, do we?**

A *Well, yes, actually. It is widely accepted now that an open management style is more effective than what used to be called the 'mushroom style'. (Keep them in the dark and throw a bucket of shit over them from time to time.) If you do it your way, you're making people bottle up the problems they've got for a once-a-year opportunity to talk about them.*

Q **Are you seriously suggesting that I ask junior members of my team what they think of my performance, despite the fact that they know nuts about our business and less about how to manage a team?**

A *Yes. It's astonishing what you can learn from such people. They can have terrific insights into the business because they're still looking at the wood not the trees. For personal insights, who better to ask than someone who has only recently formed their early impression of you? If we were you, we'd not only ask the most junior people for feedback but we'd tell an interviewer what we'd done and what we'd learnt from their reply.*

5

Talk me briefly through your history

A relatively easy one if you've done your preparation work well. The only real risk is that you'll talk about the wrong thing; so keep checking that what you're saying is relevant.

You can't play this one by ear; or if you do you're taking a huge risk. It's crucial to have prepared a few sentences about each aspect of your history that they'll be interested in.

The question cries out for clarifying questions in return. 'Is there any particular aspect of my previous experience that you want me to talk about?' This is a fair question and means that you're focusing on what they're truly interested in. It may be wise to tell them something of yourself before you ask the question; but don't go on too long without trying to find out exactly what they're looking for.

AND THIS ENABLED ME TO...

The main secret to a blistering answer to this one is to take an aspect of your working life, tell them about it and end each story with what you learnt from the

Here's an idea for you...

Get a focus into this answer that aims at the heart of the job by preparing two stories in each of the three areas of investigation: personal attributes or leadership qualities, technical/functional capabilities, ambition and future aspirations. Make sure that all the stories end up relevant to some aspect of the job description. If you get it right and all the stories fit with what they're looking for, you're starting to look uniquely like the person they had in mind.

experience. And make sure that what you learnt hits a hot button in the description of the job you're applying for. Here are some examples that show how the learning experience fits with the profile of the person they're looking for:

'University was a big step for me. I learnt how to learn, and also how to stand on my own two feet. Suddenly there was no one interested in whether I was doing the work except me. It obviously helped me become self-motivating. Since I read history, I had to write a lot of essays. This has proved very useful. I use those researching and writing skills to produce reports in my current job.'

'After two years as a first-line sales manager I was invited to take on a two-year secondment into the sales training and development department. This gave me three main things. First, I became expert in all aspects of the theory of selling. Second, I became a very experienced presenter and coach, helping everyone from rookies to seasoned professionals to learn new skills. I also pushed into new areas like remote learning and using technology in training. Finally, it gave me experience in talking to just about every division in the business. This last part gave me good exposure to the board and I formed a good idea of what happens at that level in the business.'

'I spent an interesting year as the project controller of a big IT project. This involved keeping the project control system up to date, charting progress and spotting early-warning signs that events or activities were running late. I learnt a huge amount about complex project management by working very closely with the project manager.'

For more about using your leisure time to sell yourself take a look at IDEA 37, *What are your outside interests?***

Try another idea...

Check also as you go along that you're covering the right level of detail by asking clarifying questions. 'Is this what you're looking for?' 'Do you want me to give a bit more detail in this area, or have you got what you want?'

GO A BIT PERSONAL TOO

It's always good in a brief history of you to mention some aspect of how you spend your leisure. Leave it till the end and try to get a bit of humour into it. Make sure that even though it's your leisure you're talking about, it still has relevance to the job you're applying for: 'I also run the under-eleven side at our rugby club. I enjoy the coaching side of that very much. Believe me, you learn a bit about motivation technique: particularly when you're encouraging the team to play better and enjoy the second half when it's already twenty-nine nil down.'

'*What history and experience teach us is this – that nations and governments have never learnt anything from history, or acted upon any lessons they might have drawn from it.*'
G. W. F. HEGEL

Defining idea...

23

How did
it go?

Q **I did the analysis of the job description that you suggested. It seemed to me to major on teamwork. So I made two of my longest stories illustrate my experience and skills in working as a team member. I even used a sporting example for my personal story. I was somewhat taken aback when one of the interviewers asked if I realised that I would essentially be working on my own for much of the time. Don't you think I would've done better to concentrate on demonstrating self-motivation or something like that?**

A *You could have found a way to recover by picking another story that shows how well you got on with a job alone and without a leader. Incidentally, did you check the relevance of the first story before going on to the second? If you did, that could have revealed the inconsistency earlier.*

Q **It was taking a while for me to get to the most important bit of my career in terms of doing this job when the interviewer came in and said that we should move on to another question. What do you make of that?**

A *Maybe you should have got to the main point quicker. In our experience, people do tend to go on rather long, particularly about their early days. Anyway, keep the main point in your head and use it as the answer to another question.*

6

Tell me of a time when you were risk averse

Senior businesspeople see business as a series of decisions about risk taking, or the balance between risk and return. This question is one way of checking your knowledge of and attitude to risk.

Demonstrate here how you evaluate and sometimes reject risky projects even though you may be under pressure from above or from your team to take them on.

This risk/return attitude to business is pushing down the line at present, and middle managers are expected to have a reasonable grasp of the topic and to take appropriate calculated risks.

KNOW WHERE THEY'RE COMING FROM

First of all make sure you know what sort of company you're applying to. If a company is set up to take high risks in the hope of exceptional returns, they look for people who are comfortable in that environment and willing to take a gamble.

Here's an idea for you... **It's a good idea to get a detailed example of the company's attitude to risk. Look on their website or in their annual report for a subject where they are obviously risk averse and try to develop an example in that area.**

Other companies settle for a lower rate of return and are generally considered to be more risk averse.

Your industry knowledge should mean that you are aware of the general risk profile of a company working within that industry. However, you can research how the company you're applying to sits within the industry. One clue to this is how the company's price/earnings ratio compares with the industry average. The higher it is the more risks the company is expected to take. This gives you a good question in the interview: 'I see that your p/e ratio is higher/lower than the industry average. Does this mean that you are less/more risk averse than your competitors?' This knowledge flavours your reply to this question to suit the company. You don't want to apply to the local undertakers and look like someone prepared to put a month's salary on 36 Red.

Remember that risk aversion can be both good and bad. Being risk averse is often good when you're bucking the trend or the flavour of the month; when you're not getting involved when the high rollers are riding for a fall. (The telecommunications companies who didn't get into trouble during the internet bubble at the beginning of the century were the ones who were more risk averse.) The downside of risk aversion is missing out on opportunities and then missing out on the returns.

AND SO THE DEMONSTRATION

They've asked you for an example, so give them one. You could try a financial one. 'The IT people wanted my team to implement a new computer system that had heavy backing from top management. They made impressive demonstrations of the cost/benefit argument, but I had a huge doubt that the benefits would be as large as they claimed. And I knew of course that the costs quoted would be at best the minimum they would charge. I demurred and then watched as other departments implemented the system and then complained about the returns later on. IT had to lower the price and then we went for it.' This example has all the ingredients you want: not giving in to pressure, good judgement and the proof that you were right.

Or perhaps a people-oriented one. 'A salesman with a terrific track record wanted to join my team selling to the Ministry of Defence. He also had a reputation for flashy behaviour and sailing very close to the wind. My manager urged me to take a risk with him. He believed that the salesman's flair would overcome the rather formal approach of the civil servants and serving officers that we had to deal with. Rejecting that advice, and the salesman, did me some harm. People began to mutter about me becoming as stuffed shirt as my customers. Then they took the same guy on to work with another government department. He lasted three months before the customer insisted he was taken off the account.' Or you could give a personal example, such as not buying a house that would stretch you too much if interest rates went up.

To get the balance on this question look at IDEA 25, *Where have you made your organisation take a big risk?*

Try another idea...

'*Rashness succeeds often, still more often fails.*'
NAPOLEON BONAPARTE

Defining idea...

How did it go?

Q **I thought hard about this when I was asked the question, 'Suppose you had a person in your team who was getting good results but taking terrible risks with the company's reputation. Suppose that person tended to promise more than we could deliver, what would you do?' I'd learnt in my company research that they regarded customer satisfaction and their reputation as crucial to their strategy. I decided to demonstrate appropriate risk aversion by simply saying, 'Sack them.' The atmosphere turned icy! What should I have done?**

A *You could have said that you would use the company warning procedures if the situation was really bad, but then show how you would try to enforce a business process to make sure that the employee's promises were reasonable. Say that you would also work with them on changing their behaviour. Add that, because of their results, you don't want to lose their potential, and you've covered all the bases.*

Q **A question like this came up quite late in the interview. The demeanour of the two people had made me aware that my potential boss was a greater gambler than his boss. I decided to play to the senior person and took a rather risk-averse line. After I had spoken it didn't feel right. Was I wrong?**

A *Not entirely. It's generally better to take the overall attitude of the senior person as long as it doesn't really go against your grain. You needed to balance your answer perhaps with a bit of the theory above on good and bad aspects of being risk averse. That way you are playing the ball, the process of evaluating risk, rather than the person and their prejudices.*

7

What are you like at getting difficult people to do things differently?

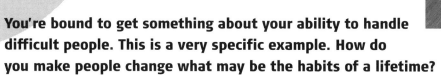

You're bound to get something about your ability to handle difficult people. This is a very specific example. How do you make people change what may be the habits of a lifetime?

It's not particularly difficult to manage enthusiastic people who are self-motivated, keep to company procedures and are great members of the team. How do you pass on your drive and energy to someone who's simply not interested or is hostile?

A difficult person resists change, moans about everyone and is happy to tell the whole team why everything is wrong. Handled poorly, they're the bad apple that ruins the barrel. You've got to demonstrate not only how you'd try to get them to accept change but also how you'd prevent their becoming a creeping cancer in the team.

Here's an idea for you...

If you don't have experience in this area find a manager who has. Get a good example of how the problem was handled and use this, attributing it to a mentor or colleague manager.

WHY ARE THEY DIFFICULT?

Sometimes people resist change because they lack some of the skills and knowledge involved in doing things differently. So you need to find out whether this is the case and at the same time show that you're willing to help these people develop. It's your job to get to understand the difficult person and why they're like what they are. Having said that, you can often get people to change by tackling them head on. Discuss not their behaviour itself but rather the impact that it's having on what they do and how other people see them.

Give an example something along the following lines. 'I had a person who absolutely refused to accept that she had to work in a different area to the one she had been in for a while. Her work was producing less and less return, and we desperately wanted her to move her attention to another product. She categorically refused to start working in an area where the younger, newer people were happily operating. I had a difficult conversation with her and she got upset; but it was useful because I found out the real problem – because of her seniority she hadn't attended the induction course where new people had found out about the new product and its potential. She was unwilling to go on a course with a bunch of rookies; so I organised for the training department to give her a one-to-one briefing on the topic and she came back changed and ready to go.'

Others are just very cynical. They see any management initiative as bound to fail and by their attitude can help to make that into a self-fulfilling prophecy. (They even have a word for it: 'BOHICA' standing for 'Bend Over Here It Comes Again'.) In this case it might be useful to say that you would make sure in the first place that they aren't right and that the change is necessary and will be effective. If this is the case, then you have two weapons – business processes and peer pressure.

Further work in this area is in IDEA 38, *Can we ask you to do a role-play and some group exercises?*

Try another idea...

'In my experience such people always stay just inside obligatory business processes. They may ignore some less significant ones but never give you a simple opportunity to prove misconduct. So I would look for how I could build the new way of working into their job; I'd try to make it impossible for them to carry out their function and resist change at the same time. I've also seen that simply ignoring them tends to leave them more and more isolated. Then peer pressure might bring them on board.'

DON'T LET THEM ROCK THE BOAT

Now demonstrate how you would prevent the difficult person infecting everyone else. 'There can be a way of making such people look for positives rather than negatives. I might try going to them frequently and asking for their advice. Their challenge becomes to look for what should be done rather than complaining about what is being done. If I can get the rest of the team cheerful and energetic, that should bring them along with the tide. If it really doesn't work and I haven't solved the problem I would try to maintain friendly relations but I would keep this very business-related. Having protected the team, I mustn't let the person get to me either.'

If the interview is going really well you could take a flyer by hinting that you've heard of head shunting where you use a friendly

'Aye, he's a difficult person, and that's on a good day.'
BOB FRASER, ICL Account Director

Defining idea...

headhunter to attract the person somewhere else. But be careful with HR people in this area; if a case like this is not handled within the rules it could lead to an unfair dismissal claim or to the duped company suing.

How did it go?

Q **I got a brilliant example of this from an old mate and told the story pretty well to the interviewer. She looked disappointed and asked if I didn't have experience of my own. So the strategy didn't work, did it?**

A *Sorry, we should have said that you preface the story by admitting that you haven't come across this problem very much. Word it in such a way as to suggest that your leadership and drive prevent it happening in the first place. It's another example of turning a potential flaw, lack of experience, into a virtue, your energy rubbing off on your team.*

Q **I answered this question in pretty much the way you suggested. When I explained that I would keep a certain distance from the person to stop them getting me down, they countered by suggesting that this might cause the person to form a clique. Are they right?**

A *Possibly, but this is not necessarily a bad thing. If their clique goes across functional borders you should be able to recruit other managers whose people are being subverted into helping to solve the problem.*

8

Will you promise to see this project through to the end?

This is an easy question to answer if there is only one person in the room – the potential line manager. It's more difficult if you have to make a response that pleases two or more people looking for different things.

You frequently need to create dual answers to questions to ensure that you are not turning one person off while you completely satisfy another.

We'll look at the three areas of investigation that interviewers are probing and then at the people most likely to be doing the probing. When you understand that, it's much easier to form such double-edged answers and anticipate the questions that belong in each area. You can then judge the direction and tone of your answer.

Here's an idea for you...

Find someone who is familiar with each of the three areas of investigation and ask them what sort of questions they use to probe for information. Nothing teaches you more than hearing things from the horse's mouth. You can also use an open question like, 'What sort of thing turns you on to a person in an interview – and what turns you off?'

WHO'S LOOKING FOR WHAT?

Let's identify the three areas of investigation: leadership qualities, functional/technical abilities and future potential. Leadership qualities are the attributes that define you. This area asks the question, 'What are you intrinsically good at?' Technical/functional abilities concern the knowledge and experience you will bring to doing the job. The question here is, 'Can you do the job?' Future potential is exactly what it says: 'Are you the sort of person we want to hire? Will you be a good resource that we can promote? Do you have the legs that will enable you to make a larger and larger contribution to the organisation?'

Now think about the people – the HR department, the boss (the potential line manager) and senior managers. You can expect the HR person to be mainly focused on the first area, the boss on the second and the senior manager on the third. So, it is vital that you know beforehand exactly who is going to be there.

You will need to tailor any response you're about to give to meet their different needs. It's easier if you can take this into account in your preparation.

YES, NO AND MAYBE

So, the answer to this question has to demonstrate energy and drive to the HR person, that you'll get the bloody job done to the line manager and that you are ambitious to the senior manager: 'I like to work in an environment where there is an aim that the whole team is striving for. I always want to see things through – completing projects gives me my main job satisfaction; but I'm always aware that the needs of an organisation change and am prepared to go where I am most needed.' You get the idea.

A question frequently asked at the end of an interview goes, 'Is there anything about you that you think we've missed?' This is a free hit question and allows you to throw a parting shot into the area where you think you've been least convincing. 'Well, I hope you've seen enough to convince you that I've got the right attitude and enthusiasm, and you've certainly probed around my knowledge and experience to know that I can get the job done. I wonder if I've got over to you how keen I am to join your organisation. Your culture and relaxed way of doing things feel ideal to me, and I think I could develop a great career here to both our benefits.'

Probably the most important interview you'll have is the one with your prospective line manager. In most cases these will be one-on-one meetings. IDEA 19 looks at a question that exemplifies what's going on in that interview, *What's your definition of the ideal relationship with your boss?*

Try another idea...

'*A statesman is a politician who places himself at the service of the nation. A politician is a statesman who places the nation at his service.*'
GEORGES POMPIDOU

Defining idea...

How did
it go?

Q **I was in an interview for a technology job with two people, the senior manager in charge of the project and the project manager, a very technically oriented woman. She asked a technical question and I answered it from some very recent experience in the same technical area. She then told me my approach was wrong and talked about techniques that are out of date. I sensed the other guy didn't like her much and so I took her on a bit, by suggesting that what I had said would in fact work. I didn't get the job. Why, when I was actually right?**

A *We suspect you'd already lost before this part of the conversation took place. Her saying you were wrong suggests to me that she'd already made up her mind. Replay the conversation in your mind and see if you can identify at what earlier point you think she turned against you. If I'm right, and you're right about the other bloke not liking her, you might as well have gone for the jugular and explained why she was out of date. But it would be a bold senior manager who imposed a technical person on a technocrat.*

Q **I'm a woman and I keep getting asked the question, 'Are you planning to have a family?' Often it's not as bold as that, but hinted at in various ways. Is it true that women managers are more likely to dislike a positive answer to that question?**

A *It seems to be, yes. Research suggests women are harder on other women in this regard. Some women advocate saying 'no' even if it's a lie. Others work out a double answer such as, 'Possibly, but such things are in the future and depend first of all on success in my career. I certainly have no intention of taking time off just when I'm starting to make a contribution to the organisation.'*

9

Could you send me your CV please?

Your CV is a selling document and the product it is selling is you. You want someone who is trying to fill a new post to reach for your CV and like what they see.

The 'inside salesperson' is salesperson's jargon for someone who supports the salesperson and advances their case internally when the salesperson isn't there. A CV can do the same thing for a person seeking a job or promotion.

PRESENT IT WELL

Nowadays it is very easy for the CV's presentation to be first class, so anything else is an inside suicide note. Make sure it is also in pristine condition, every time.

An actor of the old school with a booming voice that made every phrase sound as if it were by Shakespeare was frequently out of work and always short of money. He used to go around the local shops trying to cash cheques. One day he tried four or five places and got four or five polite refusals from shopkeepers who knew him.

Here's an idea for you... **Keep your CV consistent with the job you're applying for. You may have to tailor it for different jobs. Once you have written the CV, get as many people as possible to look it over for you. Take it to business managers who hire people into their teams, and to someone who works in HR. In the end the same document has to work for both.**

By this time the cheque looked somewhat crumpled and dilapidated. His final try was at the laundry. 'Would you be so good as to cash me a small cheque?' he said. 'I'm sorry,' came the reply, 'but we still have an old one of yours that bounced.' 'Oh well,' said the actor, 'could you at least iron the bloody thing?'

Nowadays, of course, it's highly likely that you'll send in your CV by email, but if they want hard copy make sure it's highly presentable, not like a well-thumbed cheque. It is up to you how complete your CV is, but you don't have to put anything on it that may damage your case. You can probably miss out the wrong job that only lasted six months, and a slight exaggeration of your role in your present company may help your chances of getting a more senior job with a competitor, as long as it's not too far from the truth. You'll have to substantiate it. Make the document fit in with the style of the job, formal and professional for the accountants, witty and outrageous for creative jobs.

WHAT'S IN IT?

Following your name in bold, write a first paragraph describing who you are and what you're like: 'An energetic IT project manager, with wide experience in complex projects, predominantly focused on bridging the gap between the business managers who generate the profits and the IT department who support their endeavours. Experienced influencer and coach. Decisive, commercially focused and passionate about service and quality. A proven record of delivering first-class results in major global companies.'

Now put down your career history starting with your current job and going back to your first. Make sure that each job has an illustration of the impact you had on the results, preferably financial, of the organisation you were working for. Don't just say what you did; say what it did for the company. Then put in your personal details, education and qualifications, contact numbers and addresses and outside interests.

Look at the consequence of CV exaggeration in IDEA 39, *It says in your CV that you took control of your last project when the project manager went sick. How did that go?*

Try another idea...

Research shows that a quarter of all CVs contain lies. Most firms don't test skills; so it's possible to get away with an exaggeration of your computer or other skills, but still quite dangerous. The humiliation when your boss uncovers your deception will give you a very rough start. A lie never ceases to be a time bomb, and it's so easy to forget what you said if it wasn't the truth.

If the job seems ideal for you, and you seem ideal for the job, don't pretend to meet a criterion set by the employer, rather work out in your preparation why the criterion is unnecessary and/or how quickly you could become able to fulfil it in any case. Use a covering letter to accentuate the particular experience you have to do the job. If there is an attribute in the advert or job description that you don't have, point the gap out and balance it with a strength that you do have that more than compensates for the lack. That way, forewarned by the letter they're more likely to read on when they hit the gap in the CV.

'The only end of writing is to enable the readers better to enjoy life, or better to endure it.'
SAMUEL JOHNSON

Defining idea...

How did it go?

Q   I have written a brilliant CV and presented it beautifully. Then along comes their application form and I have to handwrite the CV. My terrible handwriting makes my application form look as though it were written by a ten-year-old. Any tips?

A   *Maybe you could ask the company to send you the document in by email so that you can fill it in electronically. Possibly you could scan it? Otherwise just depend on the fact that good handwriting is not a requirement of the role, which it rarely is.*

Q   Why are you on about a covering letter? I sent my CV in with a compliments slip. Surely the CV speaks for itself.

A   *The covering letter is the thing that's read first, so get it right! You can be pretty sure if you've kept it short that it will be read from start to finish. This is more than can be said for the CV itself. The letter also acts as the bridge between your standard CV and this particular role.*

10

What do you think about team targets?

You will almost certainly get a question that asks you to explain what you think about the power of teamwork.

The whole is greater than the sum of the parts. Most projects and departments see themselves as teams or sub-teams within teams.

Although this sounds a simple question, we can use it to illustrate the need, from time to time, to ask a clarifying question. Make sure that you know what they mean by 'team targets'. They could be talking about team objectives and/or bonuses or privileges earned as a result of team performance.

I'M A TEAM PLAYER

Start from your assessment of the attributes of a good team player. 'When a team is really working well everyone performs their job in a way that helps other team members to operate efficiently. Apart from that, good team members recognise their responsibility to make the workplace a friendly and pleasant place to be. In this way everyone is working for the common good. Good teamwork also produces a sense of pride that can be the envy of other teams – and makes it easier to attract good people into the team.'

Here's an idea for you...

Find a good example of a team of talented sportspeople and notice how the coach and the players talk about the team all the time. When an interviewer asks, 'How does it feel to have scored the winning goal?' the scorer always uses the word 'team' in their answer: 'Well, the whole team felt great because we feel it was a just reward for how well we had all prepared and how hard we have all worked.' At the time of writing the English cricket team is a brilliant example of this. Take a note of how they talk and see if you can get that into the interview.

If they're considering you for a team leader role, add something about that. 'It's part of the team leader's role to make sure the team is aiming in exactly the right direction by, for example, understanding what the whole team should be trying to achieve. Good team leaders also take advice from members of their team about how things can be done differently and better. A good team leader is able to understand each of the individuals in the team and to allow them to really use their strengths.'

INDIVIDUAL ACHIEVEMENT IS IMPORTANT TOO

In terms of objectives and rewards, go for a balance. 'I certainly think the team should know how their leader is going to be judged and this gives them the team target. It's good for team spirit when everyone can see a steady progress towards success. When they do achieve success it's a good idea that there should be a team reward, financial or otherwise. But I don't think that even good team members believe that everyone has made the same contribution, so there always has to be some differentiation between individuals. I guess I'm saying that you need a balance.'

Supplementary questions could go into potential conflict between team members. The interviewers might ask, 'Isn't it normally the case that the egos of individuals get in the way of such a sharing, caring way of working together?' Here's a way of answering that and getting a point across about your flexibility: 'Not necessarily. It is possible to promote an atmosphere where one team member can make a suggestion to another directly without upsetting them. This is much better than an atmosphere where the only way you can give advice to a colleague is through the mutual manager. Having said that, yes, some egos will never take such implied criticism and will only take direction from above. You've got to single out how people work and deal with them accordingly.'

The teamwork theme continues in IDEA 13, *Would you mind taking a simple test to see how you might fit in with your colleagues?*

Try another idea...

Be ready for the question, 'What would you say is your contribution to the team?' Prepare something like, 'I'm normally the one who suggests a process that keeps us on track and ensures that we hit our deadlines.' Don't forget that it's a whole team that's forming an assessment of you. When the receptionist asks you where you've parked and then asks you to move your car, simply smile and comply. They're going to tell people what they thought of you.

'To harness and take full advantage of team power, the individual brains and personalities involved must be encouraged to collaborate. Giving stretching goals to a team will encourage it to work collectively and introduce a sense of urgency – potentially eliminating bureaucracy as it concentrates on getting positive results in the shortest possible time.'
ROBERT HELLER, British journalist

Defining idea...

How did
it go?

Q **I was using some of this to answer a teamwork question and I could see that the line manager was becoming sceptical. I tried to get back to the individual/team balance but before I'd finished he burst in with, 'Don't you ever find that you just have to tell someone what to do?' I felt I'd blown it. Where do you think I went wrong?**

A *You did well to recognise the impending problem and recovery here is probably not too difficult. There is a kind of manager who, like the famous American football coach, believes that 'nice guys finish last'. Think about the words you're using to explain teamwork and make sure you're not sounding as though all the team members will be saints. Incidentally, the actual question he raised is a breeze. The answer is, 'Yes, you can't call a collaborative planning meeting when the canteen's on fire.'*

Q **I'm thinking of suggesting a team target in an interview for a project manager's job. I fear the criticism, 'Doesn't that mean that poor performers will get the same reward as your best player?' It's a fair point, isn't it?**

A *Yes it is. Think through the balance of individual reward versus team reward and find a solution that prevents this outcome. In your situation, since you know what the project is, you can be quite specific. In practice, everyone would have to perform to achieve the team bonus – which means that the team has to help any poor performer to improve.*

11

How do you go about managing projects?

At some point you're going to have a somewhat technical discussion about the nitty-gritty of the job you're applying for. Make sure you get the detail right for the audience you're speaking to.

Interviewers want to hire interesting people who can steer clear of jargon when required, and display a personality that will contribute to the atmosphere of the working place. They don't want to hire crashing bores.

It's quite possible that someone, probably the potential line manager, will want to have a detailed technical discussion with you. If it's a one-on-one then that's fine. Go with the flow and enjoy talking to a fellow enthusiast. We're using this example to point out the pitfalls of such a discussion when other people, HR maybe or a senior manager, are also present.

Here's an idea for you... **Work out how to explain your job to a layperson in 100 words. Remember you've got to explain it in a way that shows that you have a wealth of knowledge and experience behind this simple statement which makes you a reliable resource to get the job done. Done that? OK, try it out on a few people. Teenagers are a good bet, since you can measure their concentration span in nanoseconds. When you've made that work, reduce it to fifty words.**

FIND THE CONNECTION

You've got to say enough, of course, to prove that you have the technical ability to do the job. But leave any detail about that until after you've presented the answer in a way that shows the bridge between what your function is and how the organisation succeeds. We'll use the project management question to illustrate this idea, but it works for any function.

A project, or any department or function come to that, has its internal issues. You have to get the team to carry out the function and meet its objectives. But what outside managers are interested in is the interface where the project contributes to or harms the success of the organisation. They're also interested in the project when it impacts on other parts of the organisation. These are the bridges you're looking for when it comes to describing to non-technical people how you'll go about the job. In selling terms you're looking for the 'benefits' your function brings to the party.

So, 'At the outset I develop the objectives of the project and spend whatever time it takes to get all the stakeholders' agreement that we've got them right' is much better than, 'While not a perfect critical path analysis engine, Microsoft Project can be used to control the project and it has the benefit that most people are used to using it.'

Similarly, 'I'd talk to as many managers with relevant experience as possible to work out the resources we'd need during the project' is much better than, 'Once you've got the action plan the resource plan is quite straightforward. All you have to do is to reproduce the action plan as a resource plan.'

There's a link here with another question to which you could give a reply as long as the Reith Lectures. It's in IDEA 33, _Tell me about yourself._

Try another idea...

KEEP IT VERY, VERY SIMPLE

The lurking snake in this type of question is the fact that you're probably going straight into your comfort zone. You've got the qualifications to do the job, you've had the training to do the job and you've got experience of doing the job; so it's a whole lot easier to spend time on this bit than on tricky questions about subjects such as managing difficult people or making sure the customer drives your strategic plan. So we go on and on and on.

There's another useful technique here to keep things simple. Give them the simplest possible explanation of how you manage a project. Then ask them if they want more detail. In this example it could be as simple as, 'Planning a project needs forward thinking: who and what do I need to get the job done? It also needs backward thinking: if it's got to be finished by the end of the year what needs to be done and when?'

'A healthy male adult bore consumes each year one and a half times his weight in other people's patience.'
JOHN UPDIKE, US novelist

Defining idea...

How did it go?

Q **I know exactly what you mean with this one. But what you're suggesting doesn't work. I had a very difficult time in my last interview with a technical person and her boss's boss. I tried to give 'bridge' type answers but every time she brought me back to the detail of what I did in my last job and what I would do if offered this job. I could see that the senior guy was losing interest: he was starting to read a report he'd taken out of his briefcase. How could I have stopped this?**

A *You've got to grasp the nettle here. Ask a question of the senior person like, 'Am I going into too much detail for you?' They may say, 'No, no, carry on.' In which case you do. Or they may decide to move on. Remember that all your competitors will have had the same problem and some will have happily gone into huge detail and completely turned the senior person off.*

Q **It's not possible to digest my complex job into 100 words let alone fifty. What am I supposed to do?**

A *Don't forget that politicians and generals only need the answer to six questions such as 'Do we have enough fuel to carry out the campaign?' in order to decide whether to go to war or not.*

12

How ambitious are you?

How do you explain that your career path is shaped like a bullet but that you realise you have to get your head down and do this job well and thoroughly? Be honest and enthusiastic but mainly keen to prove yourself in the job you're applying for.

The key person here is the most senior person involved in interviewing you. They're the ones looking for talent to join their organisation, not just someone to do a job.

This question has many guises. Here are a few: 'Where do you see yourself in five years' time?' 'In an ideal world what job would eventually fulfil your dreams?' and even, 'When do you expect a promotion?'

THE SKY'S THE LIMIT

Start from an honest and reasonable answer to the question. 'Well, I certainly want to move forward and have a career that makes good progress. I know that my career will depend first and foremost on doing well in the job I go into. As I do that job I'll also become a more knowledgeable professional in this organisation and in this

Here's an idea for you...

'Where do you want to be in five years' time?' is not a bad question to ask yourself. If you have a clear career path in your head you'll handle questions like this better. Supposing that each job will last for a minimum of eighteen months and probably more like two years, the question prompts you to ask yourself about the next two moves after this job. With such a thought in your head you're well equipped to check the feasibility of this plan during the interview.

industry. This will allow me to focus my energies and skills in the areas that are key to the success of the company. I think it'll take a couple of years to get into that position and at that point I'll have a much more informed view of what is possible. But my starting point is that I'm looking to get ahead.'

The key is to show that you are ambitious but not arrogant enough to know exactly where you want to be. There are some uncertainties, not the least of which is that as yet you don't really know where the key jobs in the organisation lie. This makes a good finish to your answer: 'What do you think over the next few years will be the crucial areas for your organisation to exploit?' There's not a lot else you can say here, but it's an excellent opportunity to ask questions and get them to talk about prospects in their company in general and your prospects in particular.

DON'T LOOK KEENER THAN THE JOB JUSTIFIES

Sometimes this question is asked for the opposite reason. Some jobs, particularly in small organisations, don't offer an obvious career path or opportunities for advancement. Here's an example:

A small training company offers a course to qualified solicitors to keep their legal knowledge up to date. The lecturers are all lawyers. They are looking for a receptionist/administrator to help prepare the rooms, welcome clients as they come for the course and provide the refreshment at breaks and lunchtime. Apart from getting more involved in preparing visual aids and handouts, there is no real career progression. Who're they going to take on for the job? They don't want a complete deadbeat, someone who will settle for the job for life. Such a person won't do a good job with the clients if they just feel that their job is to make the tea. But the company has nothing further to offer. If a job like this suits you for a period of time then go for it and tell them just that. 'I want to get into a more senior job, perhaps in a solicitors' partnership. This job is ideal for me to learn about the people and the profession, particularly because I'll meet a lot of different people from different firms. I'm happy to spend, say, a couple of years doing this and then if I have to move on to get ahead I'll consider doing so. Is that a sensible plan?' Finishing with the question puts the whole issue on the table. Either you've got it dead right or they're looking for a complete deadbeat.

Another good career-oriented question is IDEA 41, *Give me an example in your career where you felt like giving up and did.*

Try another idea...

'Ambitious young people should be reasonably patient and hold the success of the company as more important than their own success.'
SIR JOHN EGAN, British executive

Defining idea...

'You cannot leave you career development solely to your employer – he just is not good enough to manage this for you!'
NEVILLE BAIN, New Zealander executive

Defining idea...

How did it go?

Q **I had quite a long conversation on this topic with my potential boss and a more senior manager who seemed very interested in me. It became clear that the former didn't like my talking about the future; he kept coming back for reassurance that I wanted to do the job we were discussing. I felt a bit torn. What should I have done?**

A *Probably pretty much what you did. Continue the conversation about the future with the senior person and keep reassuring the line manager. It sounds as though the senior person has plans in mind for you, so go with it. If, and it seems unlikely, the line manager goes against you because of your ambition their boss will probably find you something else.*

Q **My ambition is actually to come out of business at an appropriate time and go full-time into politics. I think a future manager would be impressed by that ambition. Do you think I should tell them?**

A *Not if you want to get the job. Everyone thinks, and they're probably right, that aspiring politicians dedicate a huge part of their life to getting elected, doing party business and so on. Rightly or wrongly, potential employers are going to think that you will give the job second place.*

13

Would you mind taking a simple test to see how you might fit in with your colleagues?

Despite the fact that you haven't sat a test since you were at school, there's no need to feel concerned. You need to understand a bit about the tests and limber up your brain.

Bear in mind that the test is only one part of the process. But it's still a good idea to give it your best shot.

There is an intrinsic fallibility in making decisions based on interviews. The rapport that does or doesn't exist between interviewer and interviewee can lead to the wrong conclusion. This is particularly so if the interviewer is poor at the job. That's basically why recruiters use tests.

Here's an idea for you... Have a look at one or two of the big test companies. (Google 'personality tests' will give you a good few to choose from.) The site of SHL, a big player in this area, has a lot of useful information under the title 'Candidate Helpline'. Well worth having a look at the day before the test.

JUST WHO ARE YOU?

One type of test is the personality test. The good news about these tests is that there are no right or wrong answers and they're rarely done against the clock. The recruiter is generally looking for some further evidence of whether or not you will fit the role and the company and, of course, whether it will fit you.

The only thing to do here is to be honest. Answer the questions as accurately as you can and you'll probably enjoy it. (Women's magazine editors are well aware of our partiality to ticking boxes if it's going to tell us something about ourselves.) Don't try to make out you're different from who you are. If you do, you'll be caught out in one of three ways: the test will pick it up, the test results won't fit with the data on you from the interview or you'll be offered the job on false pretences and will be found out when you're in the role. Be proud of who you are and represent yourself in a straightforward way. Anyway, if you try to second-guess what they're looking for, you'll probably get it wrong and do both sides no good.

Your answers will typically be looked at against a norm table of hundreds of people who have done the same test and a 'profile' will emerge which shows how you compare with the 'norm'. There is no right or wrong profile per se. The company will seek to establish whether your profile matches what they need for a particular role now and in the future. Typically, it will explore areas like your sociability, ability to manage in a stressful situation, degree of inventiveness, and attitude to working in a team.

HOW ARE YOU ON ROCKET SCIENCE?

The other type of test is an ability test. Although psychologists would deny it, ability tests measure some aspects of your intelligence. Again, your responses will be compared with a norm group so the company can see if you work with facts, figures and data more effectively than x% of the population. It's important to get the accuracy/speed balance correct, since most of these tests are timed. Try not to sacrifice accuracy for speed. Most testers would prefer to see ten correct answers out of eleven rather than ten right out of twenty. However, don't take too long about it. If you only answer ten out of twenty you can't get more than 50%. As usual, forewarned is forearmed. Find out from the HR people whether they're going to ask you to do a test and if so which one. They probably won't answer the second question, but it's worth a pop.

Other ability tests look at your creativity or dexterity, among many other topics. There's nothing you can do about these tests except refuse to do them and not get the job. Take a few deep breaths, keep calm and concentrate hard. Sorry to be like teacher here, but do read the questions ever so carefully. If you're going to be wrong, be wrong because you don't know, not because you read the question too quickly.

You've done the company a service by sitting the test; they must do you the courtesy of giving you feedback. If they don't offer it ask for it, politely but firmly. It can be invaluable feedback for your future. This is crucial if you sit the tests before the interview. You do rather have one arm tied behind your back if you don't get feedback from the test.

IDEA 35, *Would you be surprised if I told you that my colleague found you a bit arrogant?* continues the theme of personality.

Try another idea...

'**When you do Shakespeare they think you must be intelligent because they think you understand what you're saying.**'
HELEN MIRREN, British actress

Defining idea...

How did it go?

Q **You say that the test is only one part of the process; but I know for a fact that because of a test I was turned down for a promotion. Isn't this a real danger?**

A *Fair point. It's true that if other things are equal the test could tip the balance. It's probably quite rare that this occurs, but it may have done in your case. Ah well, nobody said life was fair.*

Q **I asked for feedback and they just said that it wasn't company policy to give any, and that was that. What else could I do?**

A *Try not to leave it like that. If you haven't succeeded face to face, send them a letter explaining the importance of the test results to you for your future. Maybe write the note to a senior person. After all, they can change company policy.*

Q **I've found out what the test is and I've done it before. Should I own up because I know what they're looking for?**

A *Not if you want to get the job, mate!*

14

Why do you want to work for this company?

Time to put on display the huge amount of research you did to get ready for this interview.

All interviewees know a lot about themselves and their aspirations. Only a few have the competitive edge of knowing a lot about the organisation and its aspirations.

There are now so many sources of information about businesses that you should be able to do a thorough analysis in a fairly short period of time.

WHAT DO YOU NEED TO KNOW?

Here are the headings:
- industry sector
- aims and strategy
- company/divisional structure
- financial performance last year
- main customers and competitors
- products and people.

Here's an idea for you...

To prepare more deeply for this question you can use SWOT analysis of their situation. Take the mission statement or aims and objectives you got from the report and ask the question, 'In terms of achieving that objective what are the company's Strengths, Weaknesses, Opportunities and Threats?' This will give you good ammunition for demonstrating knowledge and some good questions to ask about the company and its plans.

Find the website of someone who analyses this industry sector. That will give you a good overview and identify the organisation's place in the scheme of things. Then phone the company and ask for a hard copy of their annual report – they're used to being asked for them. The hard copy is better than the web version because you can see how glossy the report is, or how thrifty, or how environmentally friendly – all good clues. You'll discover the aims and strategy in the chairman's statement and the chief executive's report. The structure will be clear from the divisional reports that follow in the report. Note the overall structure and then read carefully about the part you're trying to join. It's only high level; but that's exactly what you need to answer this question.

There's a summary of the organisation's financial performance in the chairman's and finance director's statements. It would be good to be able to say, 'Your profitability is still growing well, compared both with last year and with the rest of the industry.' If you're going for a finance job, of course, you'll need to do all the financial ratios.

Most annual reports talk about the main customers they're proud of. It's good to have a success story from among these to talk about: 'You certainly did no harm to your reputation when Powergen spoke about the Dublin project.'

It's easy enough to find out about the company's products and services. You need to know the whole breadth of what they do. It's good if you can find out something about their

We look at this question from a job/person fit in IDEA 15, *So, why do you want this job?*

Try another idea...

reputation for treating their people. This helps you to know whether you want to work for them and gives you a nice compliment to pay them during the interview.

We recommend you look at two of their competitors, either by obtaining their annual reports or by visiting their websites. If you can experience the company from a customer's point of view, for example in retail, then you should certainly do so.

RELATE YOUR KNOWLEDGE OF THE COMPANY TO THE JOB

Start with the sector: 'You're in the gas sector, which is still a pretty exciting place to be. The market's growing and companies in the industry are still jockeying for position in the new competitive environment.' Now move on to the company. It's great to start with a quote: 'Your Chairman said, "The Group's excellent performance has been combined with major progress in the establishment of a culture that seeks continual operational improvements, high service standards and, above all, safety." These are all values I share and, since I'm applying for the job of safety supervisor in Sector 7G, I particularly like the emphasis on safety. The financial strength is attractive too; I want to work somewhere that can afford to keep up with the huge amounts of capital investment you need to put in just to stand still – plus some for innovation.

'For also knowledge itself is power.'
FRANCIS BACON

Defining idea...

59

According to the Gas Producers Council, a lot of investment still needs to go into offshore safety, for example.'

Keep the answer to the company itself; don't go into the attraction of the job unless they ask you to do that. You're trying to keep yourself out of this reply and concentrate on something you know they're vitally interested in – their own company.

Finally, ask a question to get them talking about the same thing: 'I wasn't sure from what I could read about you whether your ventures abroad are likely to expand or not. Can you tell me that?'

Q   **That's all very well for a big public company. I'm going to see a little training company who haven't even posted their last year's accounts with Companies House. How do I do all this for them?**

How did it go?

A   *You'll have to come clean and ask them for anything they can give you: brochures, company profiles, newspaper articles and so on. You can still research their industry. How do little players fare? Who are the big boys they'll be competing against? Would it be possible to talk to one of their customers? The latter are a great source of information and often happy to talk about their experience. It'll knock the interviewer's socks off if you give them feedback they were unaware of from a customer. If you can't get what you need by research, make a note and ask about it at the interview.*

Q   **I used this stuff and it went down really well. The only time I stumbled was when I said something that was out of date. We talked at cross-purposes for a while until they understood what had gone wrong. Anything I could have done to avoid that?**

A   *They're the experts and they're bound to know much more than is published. You ought to check their website or the site of a financial newspaper to get the most recent information about them.*

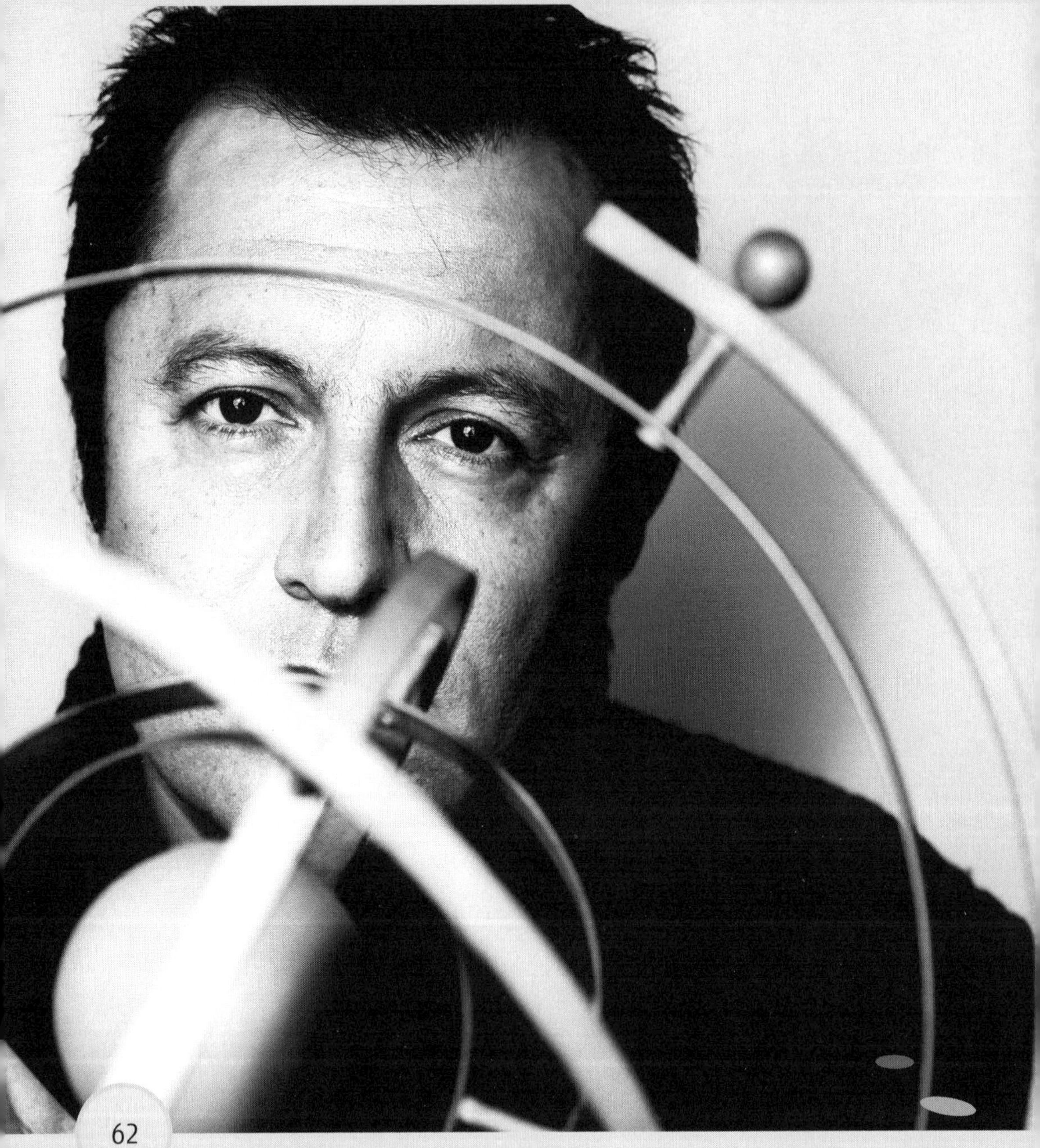

15

So, why do you want this job?

Turn a question like this into a selling opportunity by using a double answer – balance what you'll get out of the job with what they'll get out of hiring you.

It should be reasonably easy to answer this one as long as you're going for the right job. If it's very difficult, then ask yourself if this is the right employer for you before you go in.

An employer wants people to join them with enthusiasm for the challenges they're about to face. Similarly you want to get into an environment where your working life gives you joy rather than grief. Research and good self-insight will give you the right answer to achieve both aims.

WHAT'S IN IT FOR ME?

It's probably best to start the dual answer with the straightforward answer to the question. It's another question that depends on your research. You've got to be able to reply in terms of the company's attributes as you find them. It doesn't really matter what the situation is; you can still paint it as ideal for you. 'Most people want to work for the market leader; I could use your name with pride' could

Here's an idea for you…

This question really is one to prepare for carefully. The time will never be wasted, since this question will always crop up in one way or other. The best way to prepare is to find someone to role-play the interviewer and then try out with them the actual words you're going to use. If you can get someone in the same industry that would be best, but anyone with good experience of organisations or business should be able to help.

equally be, 'I like the way you've made such progress in your industry over the last few years. A growing company like yours suits my energetic way of working. I really enjoy success.'

Now try to get in something about their reputation. 'I understand that you can offer me a stable, challenging and inspiring work environment – you certainly have that reputation. I think it's the sort of environment that brings out the best in me.'

Now compliment the company on what it actually does. 'Many people regard your products and services as the best around. It's a pride thing again; I like to work for someone who is passionate about service and quality. I think we share those values and that I would enjoy fitting into your team.'

AND WHAT'S IN IT FOR THEM?

Your unique selling proposition is you and your skills and experience. Try to work out a way of illustrating that everything you've done points at you being the right person for them. Perhaps start from specific experience. For a team leader in credit control: 'My experience in the credit control department of a builders' merchants was, frankly, a hard school. The building industry is always suffering from companies going under. I know about collection periods, credit ratings calculated from company reports and, of course, I've heard every excuse under the sun for not being quite ready to issue the cheque. I think that as team leader I would be able to help others to learn from that experience.'

Now relate the specific skills to the goals of the organisation. 'I understand the benefits to you of getting payment in on time or even before time because I've controlled cash flow for an organisation and seen the impact it can have on profitability.'

If the job you're going for involves a degree of creativity you could use IDEA 28, *Tell me of a time when you generated a creative solution to a problem* to give you some more ammunition.

Try another idea...

You can also be more open about your skills where you're sure they're appropriate. For a production manager: 'I've always scored well in problem solving and from what you've said you need to find some new ways of cutting down the waste at the end of the production line.'

Something more personal can emphasise your uniqueness. For a training deliverer: 'The fact that I've done a bit of amateur dramatics helps me to understand the "performance" side of running a training course.'

Now bring the three things together: 'So you see why I was excited when I saw your job ad; you seem to need a person with pretty much the experience, skills and interests that I've developed.'

'And so my fellow Americans: ask not what your country can do for you – ask what you can do for your country.'
JOHN F. KENNEDY

Defining idea...

How did
it go?

Q **I've thought long and hard about this. There's rather a good job in a company that's not doing very well. I think part of the problem is that their values don't include a focus on teamwork. They have a reputation for 'hire and fire' and come over as a bit 'every man for themselves.' When they ask this question should I point out that while I'm not sure I share their current values I think I can introduce some new ones that will help to improve their performance?**

A *Possibly. Our first reaction to this was 'NO, wait until you've got the job and then sell the changes that you think they need to make.' But on second thoughts you could be right. Depends if you think that someone in the room is thinking the same way as you, in which case go for it. You could get the pleasant surprise of one of them telling you that they know they need to change in this area – in which case your preparation is ideal. (Sorry to be sceptical, but you should also bear in mind the words in script font at the top of this Idea.)*

Q **I'd like to end this answer with a bold statement. Can I say that I would like to be in my boss's position within two years – in order to demonstrate my ambition?**

A *Yes, but choose the words carefully. You're trying to make them feel confident about you, not insecure. Try, 'Finally, I have aspirations to get to your level in the not too distant future.'*

16

How easy are you to work with?

This is the real question hidden under a number of aliases. In this part of the interview they're probing for how you work with your boss and whether you are likely to be an employee who causes problems rather than one who resolves them.

You've got to show loyalty, stability and that you will be an easy person to work with and manage.

Such a question may come towards the end of an interview when they've been watching your performance for half an hour or more. Their concern is that it is a 'performance' and they want to make sure that they understand the real you.

WHO IS THE REAL YOU?

They can ask this question in various guises. 'How do you get on with your current boss?' What they're looking for here is any sign that you will rock the boat in their department. One of the most disruptive things you can get in an organisation is a

Here's an idea for you... **Think about a colleague or friend whom you know to have been critical of and disloyal to their boss. What did they say? It might have been very open or it might have been more surreptitious. Now think about the impact that had on their team. Were they sucked into the same opinion and did they also start to express it? Did it contribute to or hinder the team's performance? This brings home the characteristics and behaviour of a person who finds it difficult to play in a team, and their potential impact.**

person who sows seeds of doubt about the competence or character of the manager or team leader. So it's a straightforward, 'Personally we get on well: he's easy to work for and I think we have achieved quite a lot together.' Try to say no more, although it's likely that they'll ask supplementary questions to get you to substantiate what you've just said. They could go close to the bone with, 'I've heard that he doesn't consult much when he's taking a decision.' Just stay with a positive attitude: 'I haven't found that.' There's little possibility that they're actually interested in the character or competence of your boss; they're just probing to see if they can get you to display disloyalty.

'How are you on accepting instructions?' An easy-to-manage person is one who likes to be given objectives and tasks that are well explained at the outset. Then they just get on with it and deliver. But they're also aware that circumstances do arise where a team leader may at short notice take them off their current task and ask them to do something else. With this question the interviewers are checking that you're a team player and that you recognise that, from time to time, your boss will give you brief directions and expect compliance. You can probably find a dual answer that covers both points. 'I like to work in an environment where the logic behind what I'm being asked to do is clear. But I understand that I won't know about all the pressures and deadlines that exist. This may very well mean that I have to get on with something without knowing all the details leading up to the directions I've been given. This is fine by me because it's just a part of working in a fast-moving competitive environment.'

WORKING UNDER STRESS

'What keeps you awake at night?' This is not a therapist's question aimed at finding out your innermost fears; it's an attempt to get to know your ability to handle stress. So answer it from a professional point of view: take it as entirely business related. 'I'm concerned by the normal things a sales manager worries about: meeting targets, eking out the budget, avoiding heavy discounting and so on. But I've handled these issues for a while and I certainly don't let them get me down.'

They want to know how well you'll fit into the culture of a company; so try IDEA 18, *What is the ideal culture that you like to find in an organisation?*

Try another idea...

'Some people think that the business term FIFO stands for First in First out; but in this organisation it stands for Fit in or Fuck off.'
Speaker protected under the Fifth Amendment of the US Constitution

Defining idea...

How did it go?

Q   I thought long and hard about this because, according to your line of logic, I displayed some very disloyal behaviour when I first joined an organisation. When I arrived, my boss was also quite new and a number of the older members of his team were very critical of him, comparing him very unfavourably with his predecessor. It was easy to join in and I did. The trouble is that they were quite right and he didn't last long. If I'd gone for an interview at the time I was working for him, should I have shown complete loyalty as you suggest or indicated that I knew what his shortcomings were? After all, not everybody's perfect and the interviewer knows it.

A   *Think about it from the interviewers' point of view. Your organisation, in its wisdom, put that bloke in charge. If they think their wisdom got it wrong and they change things, that's up to them. Your job was to help your boss, whatever he was like, to succeed. It's certainly not anyone's job to undermine him and make his failure more certain.*

Q   This stress thing. Don't you think you've gone a bit far? Surely an interviewer wants to believe that you feel something for the company as well as work for it. Surely not being able to sleep at night from time to time is a demonstration of that.

A   *Look, we're not saying it never happens; but it really shouldn't. If you have a problem at work the company has the same problem. They want you to come in next morning refreshed and ready to hug the monster. You can't do that if you've spent the whole night rattling your worry beads.*

17

What is the one thing your team would most like to change about you?

Knowing yourself, or self-insight, is crucial. The answer to this question tells the interviewers a lot about you, probably including a hint of your main weakness.

Pick the thing to be changed carefully — and turn a vice into a virtue.

Let's look first on the negative side. What they are probing for here is any trait of yours that really is a red light for them not to go ahead with you. So avoid showing them any problem that might be a deal breaker.

USE ANCIENT HISTORY

Quite a neat way of handling this is to talk about a weakness that you've had in the past, that you've overcome but that you remain on guard for. 'A manager once pointed out to me that I was causing some discomfort to my team when I acted too precipitately when they came to me with a problem. I thought about it and realised that I sometimes listened to a problem and quickly proposed a solution. I might

Here's an idea for you... **Prepare for this type of question by actually asking it of your team. 'What would you most like to change about me?' With luck what they say won't be a surprise and you can work out an answer using the templates in this Idea. Perhaps it will be a surprise, in which case you've just taken a big step forward in getting to know yourself.**

then volunteer to take the first action myself. At that point I'd pick up the phone there and then to put the action plan into progress. I talked to the team about it and they agreed that it was frustrating for them because they wanted to go away, think about the plan and sort the problem out themselves. I think I've fixed it and don't do it now; but I'm aware of the tendency and watch myself carefully in those circumstances.'

This is a reasonable answer and one that shows your ability to act on criticism. Which is pertinent to another question in the area of self-insight which often comes up: 'How do you react when your manager or a team member tells you that they don't like something you do?' Now, nobody's perfect and such criticism happens to everyone. It's crucial that you display real interest in the feedback and take some action to show that you are putting things right. There's no need, however, to suggest to an interviewer that such things happen very often.

'I've come to know that whatever the criticism that people are making, there is always something in it; so I never argue about it or attempt to justify my position. In order to learn from it, I've found that you need to talk it over thoroughly, to make sure that you're both talking about exactly the same thing. When I do that, it's normally pretty easy to modify how I behave. If I then invite them to point out any reoccurrences I find that the discussion ends up useful and amicable.'

PICK SOMETHING THEY ACTUALLY QUITE LIKE

There's another self-insight question in IDEA 44, *Would you say you're a glass-half-empty person or a glass-half-full?*

Try another idea...

This depends on your function. Every job has a bit in it that people don't like or see as a low priority. For a salesperson it's easy. No one likes doing the paperwork. Often in a rather macho way, people regard it as getting in the way of the real work – the selling work. Once again present the issue as something you know you have to continuously overcome.

'I know I have a tendency to get a bit behind with the paperwork. I also know that that can upset the office people terribly and, if left undone for long enough, can lead to missed deliveries and customer dissatisfaction. So, I've put a severe discipline on myself to keep up to date every Wednesday afternoon when a lot of my customers are closed.' Whatever your function you can probably find your version of the salesperson's paperwork.

'*The real solvent of class distinction is a proper measure of self-esteem – a kind of unconsciousness. Some people are at ease with themselves, so the world is at ease with them.*'
ALAN BENNETT, British playwright

Defining idea...

How did
it go?

Q **Oh my goodness, I did it! I talked to the team and they completely threw me. They accused me of being too quick to show frustration and even anger when I thought that someone had made a mistake or wasn't pulling their weight. I honestly thought that I was just raising my voice to make a point. Not only that, but I'm going for an internal promotion; so the interviewer may have had this feedback. What can I do?**

A *We did warn you that you might get a big step forward in self-knowledge. In the circumstances, you should probably expect a question along the lines of this Idea and choose that weakness as your example. You should be able to find an example that employs the 'use ancient history' method and shows that you know about the problem and that you're working on it. You could also try to turn this shock into a positive by telling the interviewer that you talked to the team as part of your preparation. 'They made me aware that I have to continue working on maintaining a positive attitude at all times, especially to under-performers.'*

Q **I'm a saleswoman and used the 'I'm sometimes poor at the paper-work' line. I said it quite wittily and the sales manager laughed. The HR person then grilled me about it and asked me if I understood what problems letting the admin slip can cause. By the end of that, I don't think I'd done myself any favours. Don't you agree?**

A *It looks as though your answer was dead right for the sales manager. But, since there was someone else there it would have been wiser to take a more sober approach. Perhaps make the witty remark, then quickly go on to demonstrate that you really do understand the problems created by poor paperwork.*

18

What is your ideal organisational culture?

You're sitting there; so you must have decided that you quite like what you believe to be their culture. Just describe your ideal place to work and if you've analysed them correctly you'll be describing their culture as well.

You've got to be open and honest here. If the culture's not right, you'll eventually hate the job. You really are looking for compatibility.

Regardless of how well you fit the job and the job fits you, the thing that makes the organisation successful and you happy is the culture. It's the context within which everyone works. Use the interview to check that you understand the way they work and that you'll enjoy fitting into it.

THERE'S NO RIGHT ANSWER

Let's start with an easy one. If you're a very creative person don't go for a company that's very process driven and where strict attention to the rules and the small print

Here's an idea for you...

Think about times in your career when you've been very successful and enjoyed the job at the same time. Now think about the culture you were working in. What was it about the culture that contributed to those good feelings? Now try the opposite – when you were miserable. Comparing the two should help to uncover the environment in which you really like working.

is part of their function. Much of a lawyer's job is the careful interpretation of other people's writing. Maybe not right for someone who fancies herself as an innovator. So to prepare for this question define the elements of an organisation's culture that concern you. The list below gives you some cultural attributes to help you to do this:

Bureaucratic vs. meritocratic and open. On one end of this scale is the organisation that normally promotes through length of time in the job. You can't go from level 5 to staff level 6 without working there five years. You can't get to level 6 at all unless you're a graduate. The mark of a meritocracy is that high-fliers are put into challenging positions at the first opportunity. Openness tends to go with meritocratic. (The dining rooms are often a quick guide to all this: are they segregated by seniority or does everyone muck in at the same canteen?)

Internal vs. external focus. Do you want to work in an environment where your plans are pretty much dictated by the level above you, or do you want to drive your plans by thinking about what the external customer wants?

Quality/cost balance. Do you want to work in Rolls Royce, or do you want to work for a company that's increasing its efficiency so much that they can offer good products to a mass market?

Freedom vs. process and control. Are you a risk-taking maverick who likes to spot an opportunity, go for it and ask permission afterwards? If so, you're not going to be comfortable in an environment where any step out of line is met with tutting noises. Many people are more comfortable in an organisation that lets them know precisely where they are and what their sphere of operation and influence will be.

Fun vs. serious. What does it feel like when you walk in the door and talk to people? By 'fun' we don't mean frivolous, but some organisations take themselves less seriously than others.

Open vs. closed communication. Do they give a lot of information to a wide audience, or do they inform only those who need to know?

Team vs. individual. Does the organisation operate through its teams, or through its individuals?

Now mark on a scale of 1–10 how you think the organisation you're applying to works against your list of attributes. Also mark on a scale of 1–10 how the culture suits you. Where you can't answer the question through lack of knowledge, make a note to ask a question in that area at the interview.

There's a good link here to IDEA 40, **How will you know when you've found the right job?**

Try another idea...

'**All my wife has ever taken from the Mediterranean – from that whole vast intuitive culture – are four bottles of Chianti to make into lamps.'**
PETER SHAFFER, British dramatist

Defining idea...

IS WHAT THEY DO WHAT THEY SAY THEY DO?

Sometimes companies proclaim their culture as one thing and actually act in a completely opposite way. You can check on this in the interview: 'In your company accounts it says that everyone in the organisation is encouraged to be innovative. How does that work?' If they say that their customers drive everything they do, you could ask, 'What processes do you have in place to check on the changing requirements of your customers?'

WE CARE ABOUT OUR PEOPLE!!!!

This is a frequent 'Do what I say and not what I do' area. It's amazing how often the chairman's statement in the annual report contains something like, 'In the end our greatest assets are our people and I want to express my thanks to them for all their hard work' while somewhere else in the same report it's noted that the downsizing exercise has gone well.

Q   I made a huge assumption about the organisation I was trying to get into. They talked a great talk at all levels about being a 'collection of individuals' with a lot of freedom of action. That's how I like to work. I asked a few questions and it became clear that in reality they had a lot of rules, including, would you believe, firm rules about what you had to wear in the office and out at customers'. I almost wish I hadn't probed. What shall I do with their offer now?

How did it go?

A   *We're glad you probed and found out the reality. You're now in a good position to make an informed choice. It's much better to have found out now than when you've been working for them for a couple of weeks. It's a simple question: do the other terms, conditions and career opportunities make up for working in a less than ideal culture?*

Q   I found this Idea quite difficult. It's taught me that I've been pretty happy in most cultures even though I've been in some very different ones. How can I answer the question about culture now?

A   *Emphasise your flexibility and explain that you can work well and enjoy working life in different types of organisation.*

81

19

What's your definition of the ideal relationship with your boss?

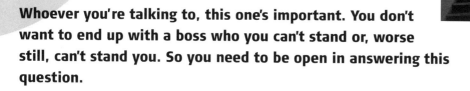

Whoever you're talking to, this one's important. You don't want to end up with a boss who you can't stand or, worse still, can't stand you. So you need to be open in answering this question.

Start from a very process-oriented view of the question. Then at the end talk personally.

The interface with your manager comes in three main areas: agreeing objectives and tasks, solving internal and external problems, and your personal and career development.

HOW DO YOU LIKE TO WORK WITH YOUR BOSS?

Start with agreeing objectives. Explain that you like a very thorough briefing on what they want you to achieve. 'I want to work for someone who is interested enough in the detail of what I do to ensure that I have a comprehensive knowledge of my project. I also like to know how my project fits into the whole divisional and

Here's an idea for you... **Although, when asked this question, it would be over-egging the pudding simply to describe the person you're talking to, it's not a bad idea to know enough about them to get a flavour of that into your answer. Try to research the actual person you'll be working for. Talk to one of their colleagues or preferably someone whose opinion you value who works for them. Plainly, this is more likely to happen in an internal promotion.**

company strategy. I much prefer tightly written objectives that make it clear whether or not I'm on the way to achieving the right results. That I always think is the first key. I can then work on the rest of the details, only bringing my boss in when something is happening that's outside my control and is going to impact on my success.'

Now think about what else you want out of them in terms of problem solving. 'I like to be able to go to my boss with a problem whenever I judge the time is right. I also like it if they expect me to come with some analysis of the problem – I tend to list the strengths, weaknesses, opportunities and threats that arise from the situation. I also like to work for someone who encourages me to come up with my own recommendations for what we should do. That preparation work should make the manager's task easier. If you don't present the problem in that way, you're just alerting them that's something's going wrong and letting them work out what to do. I expect them to give me a fair amount of protection from company politics, and I certainly hope they'll keep making sure that what I'm doing is good for the whole organisation.'

Venture a little bit now towards the relationship between the two of you. 'It's very important to me that our relationship is very open and that we can say what we like to each other without causing hurt or animosity. We need to stay positive with each other: I find that then it just works, and the relationship develops well.'

HOW DO YOU LIKE TO GET FEEDBACK?

The quick answer to this is, 'All the time, and given in a way that allows me to exploit my strengths and work on my weaknesses.'

The longer answer looks at your career development: 'I want to work in an environment where my boss expects me to do well on the job I'm doing, but knows that I'm also looking to move on and make progress. I hope that they will recommend and send me on training courses that help me to develop as a professional with a good career.'

A summary would go like this: 'My ideal manager works in an open manner and with integrity. They make sure I understand what I have to do and fully support my endeavours.'

Watch out for questions that probe for negatives, like, 'Does your current boss do anything you dislike?' Straight bat needed here: 'Well, I'm not sure that "dislike" is the right word; but she tends not to give me enough feedback. I've shared this with her and it seems to be working better now.'

This is an area where your references, particularly the one from your boss, should give a picture that's consistent with your answer. Try IDEA 42, *Is it all right if we take up your references now?*

Try another idea...

'To the ordinary working man, the sort you would meet in any pub on Saturday night, Socialism does not mean much more than better wages and shorter hours and nobody bossing you about.'
GEORGE ORWELL

Defining idea...

How did it go?

Q   **Personally I really like a boss to give me a lot of freedom and scope. During the interview with her it became clear that that is not her style. She seemed to want her people to play down a tightly controlled line. How should I have answered this question in these circumstances?**

A   *You could tell the truth and see what happens. She might not like it, in which case you won't get the job; but that may not be a bad thing. She may agree to modify her normal style if she really wants you, in which case she'll say something about that. If you really want the job, you may have to modify what you're looking for and keep your desire for freedom to yourself. Tell her that you can, if it's necessary, work within solid guidelines. You pays your money and takes your choice.*

Q   **During the meeting, I got no clear indication of the interviewer's management style. He played it very straight. I wanted to ask at the end of my answer to this question whether he fitted that description or not. Would that have been a good idea?**

A   *Yes, brilliant. Try, 'It would be good to understand how that fits with your style.' It's a nice tack because it helps to develop the two-way relationship.*

20

In your current role what are you most proud of achieving?

This is a great opportunity. Just take a good solid achievement that was down to you and tell them about it.

The only snake to avoid here is going into the detail of how you achieved something rather than sticking with the benefits you brought to your organisation, your boss and your team.

That trio – organisation, boss and team – is probably a good starting point for organising the way you present your answer. Remember that you want the interviewers to know that you personally had an idea and saw it through; but they also want to be satisfied that you're a team player. So give credit where it's due.

HERE ARE THE RESULTS

'How did your last project contribute to the company's objectives?' When answering this part of the overall question get the benefits of what you achieved as close to the bottom line of the profit and loss account as you possibly can. You

Here's an idea for you...

When you are preparing to answer this question it's a good idea to have supporting evidence. If, for example, you're not sure of the financial benefit of what you achieved your financial controller may be able to help you create a retrospective cost justification. And it's always a good idea to have a customer recommendation, whether your customer is external or internal to the organisation. It's worth asking whether they would support your mentioning them in the interview.

should also get as far as you can towards the external customer. A great answer combines the two:

'Without a doubt the implementation in our department of the new stock control system had the most impact. When I was brought in, the technical team had done a great job in getting the pilot system up and tested, and the department was quite positive about rolling it out to cover our whole operation. If there was a problem, it was simply the communication bridge between the two. Because of my experience in IT as well as stock management, I was able to coordinate things, bring the right people together at the right time and help smooth the way ahead for two talented teams. I also saw the need for some familiarisation training for some staff who were plainly apprehensive about the changes that were taking place. We completed the project within budget and about two weeks earlier than planned. The benefits to the bottom line are measured in millions and we're already getting good feedback from the stores on the reduction of stock-outs and the subsequent increase in customer satisfaction.'

Keep it at that level. Don't make the mistake of claiming as an achievement the fact that it was you who chose the software used in the project and then giving them a long exposition on just-in-time stock management.

AND DON'T FORGET THE PEOPLE

'The manager who brought me in was delighted with how it went. She told me at the outset that the system was taking up far too much of her time and that other areas in the department were starting to suffer. But perhaps the most pleasing part of the project was the party we held to celebrate the completion of the project. The whole department was on top form and rightly very proud of what we'd achieved.' Given that answer, there might be a supplementary question about project management: 'You think that a celebratory party at the end of a project is important?'

'I certainly do. It avoids the horrible feeling of anticlimax that comes after teams have put in a big effort. It allows people who have worked together for a while to say goodbye, and, of course, it gives a great platform for senior management to give the people a big thank you for what they've achieved. What we did was to combine it with a huge meeting beforehand where we agreed and documented all the things we'd learnt during the project. I actually think such an event is important for small achievements as well as big projects.'

There's more on project management in IDEA 11, *How do you go about managing projects?*

Try another idea...

'Thus, to be independent of public opinion is the first formal condition of achieving anything great or rational whether in life or science. Great achievement is assured, however, of subsequent recognition and grateful acceptance by public opinion, which in due course will make it one of its own prejudices.'
G. W. F. HEGEL

Defining idea...

How did it go?

Q **I adapted your answer to my job and gave a pretty similar spiel at a recent interview. I had good substantiation for the financial benefits; but a rather sceptical manager pointed out that the costs of the project had rocketed before I'd got there and he wondered whether the whole project had actually made a profit. I didn't handle that very well and lost some ground as a result. What could I have done?**

A *Bad luck; there's always one in every interview, isn't there? When cost/benefit analysis has gone a bit wrong, don't forget to add in what would've happened if your team had not undertaken the project at all. You can normally paint the original situation as deteriorating. The stand-by in these circumstances is to fall back on the poor customer service that existed before the work was done.*

Q **I am going to need a story like this in an interview I'm going to shortly. Trouble is that my current team is being disbanded because we're not part of the core business any more. Wouldn't you agree it's a bit difficult to point at my greatest achievement in those circumstances?**

A *Then tell them how good you've been at maintaining staff morale at a time when people could become upset and demotivated. How did you keep everyone going when they all knew they were moving on?*

21

Do you enjoy hard work?

It's a rubbish question; so hit it for six. What do they expect you to say? 'Good Lord, no, I've always tried to keep my head down and avoid the real action.'

If they mean by 'hard work' energy and drive, then, yes, you've got it in buckets.

This is a closed question, but the answer 'yes' won't do. You'll be surprised how easy it is to take a closed question like this and mould it into some points that you want to make, in almost any area you care to choose. So it's an opportunity to deliver the set pieces that you have so carefully prepared. You could go towards the 'work/life balance' or 'don't work harder; work smarter' or anything that shows you will be an energetic contributor to their enterprise. We'll look at the question as it is and then at other questions getting at the same thing.

YOU CAN ALWAYS MAKE THINGS BETTER

'I've always been enthusiastic about my work. I've generally been in jobs that I enjoy, so that makes putting the effort in quite easy. This is particularly true when I'm working for an organisation with whose objectives I can easily identify.' You can try balancing an answer like that with another benefit they're after – people who are constantly looking for ways that they and their team can do things better.

Here's an idea for you... **Find a good example of where you've looked at your or a team member's work and found a really effective procedural change that you got the company to accept. What was the benefit to the organisation of making that change? What was the benefit to the individual? Such an example is sure to come in useful for this type of question or another.**

'I do regard it as part of everyone's job to suggest improvements. When I've asked people in my team if they can see better ways that they could use to get the job done, it's amazing; in almost every case the answer is "yes". This is also true if you ask them about their interface with other parts of the organisation. They can always suggest even quite small changes that another department could make that would make their job easier and their performance more effective. So if I or other people in the team are having to work longer and longer hours, it's always worth looking for suggestions as to how we can improve the way the work gets done.'

This could lead to, 'How would you deal with a person in your team who complained continuously about how hard they had to work?' To which you might reply, 'First of all I'd take it very seriously. I'd ask them to discuss it with me and perhaps keep a record of their activities over a period of time. We'd look together for ways to reduce their workload or change our systems and procedures in some way. If I became sure that we were making unreasonable demands on the person, I'd raise the matter with my boss and try to find a solution. You have to be careful, though. I've found that some people do work hard, but don't want to change anything – not even the fact that they moan all the time about how hard they have to work.'

OTHER PROBES IN THIS AREA

'How are you at working under pressure?' To which you might say, 'Oh, I've had to handle that in all my jobs and I'm comfortable in that environment. Having said that, I try to plan ahead and avoid deadlines and crises creeping up on the team or me. That way we keep the pressure at a sensible level.'

IDEA 43, *What other roles are you considering, and how does this one stack up?* is a related question in this area.

Try another idea...

'Are you most comfortable with fairly regular hours?' Answer this one as usual with a balance: 'I'm well aware that in a competitive industry such as this you can't expect to work completely regular hours. In fact I'm not sure I'd like to have to do that. But there are some regular parts of my family life that I like to protect. For example, last year my daughter went to ballet every Wednesday evening. It suited us for me to take her and her friend to the class. I therefore agreed with my boss that I would always get away on time on a Wednesday and it worked out well.'

'Work expands so as to fill the time available for its completion.'
C. NORTHCOTE PARKINSON, British historian

Defining idea...

How did it go?

Q **I tried your advice on this one and I think it made me look as though I'm work shy. I explained how we'd found a way round some work that a colleague was doing – which gave her much more spare time. The bloke in the interview said that it sounded as if she and I were just looking for shortcuts. Did I make a mistake in the way I presented this?**

A *Well done; shortcuts are exactly what we should all be looking for as long as they don't compromise quality. Perhaps the mistake you made is in the wording 'spare time'. Could you have explained what she was able to get on with in that spare time, like finding new customers or working on the administration backlog? But we think it's bad luck to meet someone who thinks the word 'shortcut' is pejorative.*

Q **I really liked the idea of setting one day a week when I had to get away on time, and went to my boss to negotiate Tuesdays. She said that I was being unreasonable and that she couldn't give me any such guarantee. She told me that we were in business to make a profit and that meant being open when people wanted to buy. Why didn't this request work?**

A *We wonder if you were clear enough about why Tuesday was so important to you. And did you try to see it from her point of view before making the request? It would have been good if you could have proposed how it would always be feasible to cover for you on those evenings.*

22

What opinion have you formed of the people you've met so far?

This is a judgement question that invites you to show good observational skills and the ability to form an opinion about colleagues and express it positively.

Oh, and it's a chance to show a bit of tact too!

This one, or one like it, comes up quite often. There's one rule only for your reply: don't call into question anyone's competence even if you truly think it's poor. In all cases you can compliment anyone you're talking to, at least on their interviewing skills.

SUM THIS GUY UP FOR ME, WOULD YOU?

You can't completely duck the question with, 'Well it's a bit soon really; I'd need to see more of them in the real work environment before I could come to a conclusion.' Such a reply will only lead to another question in the same area and you can't go on ducking it forever. It's part of working life that we form judgements about people quickly. It's a necessary skill that gets more and more important as you go up the organisation.

Here's an idea for you...

It's quite possible, and often quite fun, to practise summing people up. Pick a colleague or a friend and get them to introduce you to their team or workmates in a way that allows you to have a short conversation with them. During that conversation try to ask questions that enable you to form a view of each one. Then discuss what you made of the people and see how well it agrees with the views of the person who knows them quite well. It'll probably improve your summing-up skills, and it'll certainly give you a hilarious half-hour over a beer.

Be as honest as possible, probably by playing the ball not the person – that is, talking about people's knowledge, experience and skills rather than their personality or style: 'I'm certainly very impressed with the depth of knowledge of the distribution business that everyone here demonstrates. I know I could learn a lot from X's experience, some of which is in a totally different area from mine. I also got the impression that Y's enthusiasm and ability to take you along with them demonstrated real skills in motivating people.'

Another good way to exploit this part of the interview is to talk about whether you would like to work with someone. Don't say it if it's not true, of course. Answering this way gives you the opportunity to ask a question that could get you some useful feedback: 'I enjoyed talking to Y; we seem to have much the same views on motivating teams. I also felt very comfortable with X; our different backgrounds gave us a lot to talk about. They've both given me the feeling that I could work with them and that I would fit into your environment.'

YOU CAN'T THINK MUCH OF HIM, SURELY?

Some quite aggressive interviewers may push you towards an indiscretion in this area, even to the point of saying, 'I have no time at all for X; I don't see how anyone can expect to run a team like she does. Her view is that the right way to act it is to tell everyone precisely what to do, with no room for any input to decision making from anyone else.'

Try to duck this one, but if they're insistent go firmly for a positive, perhaps quite long, comment: 'She and I haven't really discussed team leadership. Most of our conversation was about the distribution business, which she plainly knows like the back of her hand. I was particularly impressed by what she and the rest of the organisation are doing in identifying overseas suppliers. There's got to be room for a certain amount of risk-free arbitrage in that approach, and blah, blah, blah…'

With a bit of luck this should stop any further probing in this area. It's almost certain when they ask a question in this aggressive way that they're really probing to see if you'll take a negative position on people. There's nothing more disruptive to a team than someone bitching about other members; the interviewers want to be satisfied that you'll always stay positive about your colleagues.

Try another idea…

IDEA 16, *How easy are you to work with?* looks at interviewers who might encourage you to say something negative about your current boss.

Defining idea…

'*It is the nature, and the advantage, of strong people that they can bring out the crucial questions and form a clear opinion about them. The weak always have to decide between alternatives that are not their own.*'
DIETRICH BONHOEFFER, German theologian

How did
it go?

Q **I was in a difficult position in this regard recently and, rightly or wrongly, decided to ignore your advice. I'd had a very difficult interview with the man I would have been working for and I simply couldn't get along with him. He treated me with some disdain. I can't say for sure, of course, that he was like that simply because I'm a woman; but I couldn't see how we could work together. Later someone asked me this question and I told them in a tactful way that I hadn't enjoyed my interview with that person as much as the others. I didn't get the job. What do you make of that?**

A *Crikey! You probably did the right thing for yourself. It's obviously better that you steer clear of him – unless you want to take him on for sex discrimination. Be careful if you do: it's very difficult to make a case like this stick unless he asked a question that's illegal – such as, 'Are you planning to have a family?' which in some circumstances counts as discriminatory. If you want to help the organisation, and any other women he's going to upset, maybe you should now go back and tell them more clearly why you didn't get on.*

Q **I already know one of the interviewers quite well. Should I tell anyone who asks this sort of question that I have a lot of foreknowledge?**

A *Probably best to leave it up to them. Just give a brilliant and positive opinion; that's what they've asked you for.*

23

I see you're not a graduate. Why should we change our habit of hiring only graduates into this job?

We'll take this specific question here and add to it how you handle the fact that you are clearly less qualified than the competition.

Whatever the weakness that they probe, don't forget that they have invited you to the interview; so unless someone has blundered it's still possible for you to get the job.

It can be a good thing to ask a clarifying question at this point. 'Do you [all] think that only graduates should have this sort of job?' Once again unless someone's blundered they've got to say 'no' to this question; otherwise they're wasting their own time as well as yours. With a bit of luck one of them will be more certain that the successful candidate doesn't have to be a graduate. You may have an ally there. As you answer the question see if you can appeal to that person to help you out.

Generally, it's not your qualifications or even your experience in carrying out the tasks that'll get you the job. It's what they think of you as a person. Work out a little presentation that illustrates that you are interesting to talk to and keen to make your contribution. You'll find some way to work it into the conversation, either from your seat or using a couple of laptop slides. Some people have won jobs because they surprised everyone by giving an effective and witty presentation even though they hadn't been asked to prepare one.

IT WAS MY CHOICE

Let's look at the graduate problem. The first trick in answering it is to avoid giving them the impression that you've got to the age of twenty-seven or whatever and suddenly realised that you need some sort of proper job and the possibility of a career. No, you chose to prepare for your career not by going into further education but by doing something else. Now work out what you learnt doing whatever you did. The main reason people like graduates, even when their subject has nothing to do with the job in hand, is that they believe that graduates have learnt to learn on their own. That's what you need to demonstrate here.

Anne Scott James, a journalist with a worldwide reputation for getting herself into the right place at the right time, used the following technique to get past customs officials and guard posts. She emptied out a huge handbag on their counter in order to search for the particular documents they wanted and she didn't have. She then acted the dizzy lady, smiled a lot and was incredibly successful in getting her own way. She didn't learn that at any university.

The thing you don't learn much about at university is motivating people and overcoming people problems such as those James faced. Concentrate on examples of this. 'I think my couple of years as an assistant in a wine shop taught me a lot about customer service,

There's a linked idea about a specific lack of qualifications in IDEA 26, *Do you feel your lack of financial knowledge will put you at a disadvantage?*

Try another idea...

working as a member of a team and the importance of being disciplined and trustworthy. From my understanding this job is a lot about all of those.' (Not many university students are entrusted with taking the entire takings of the student's union bar to the bank.) If rapport is good, you could try dropping a couple of names. Richard Branson didn't go to university and neither did the President of the Save the Children Fund. (Mind you, the latter is Princess Anne.)

YOU'RE NOT THE MOST QUALIFIED FOR THE JOB

Ask a line manager what they look for in all the interviews they ever go to and they will say some variation on the following: 'I look to see whether I trust them, whether we can work with them and if they are capable of doing the job – in that order.' Not much about qualifications there. So don't despair if you are less qualified; use the interview to prove that they can't do without you and show how you will work on any weaknesses they perceive you have. Ask them also about the company policy of helping people to go to night school, get trained, assist with day release or whatever is appropriate.

'My only qualification for being put at the head of the Navy is that I am very much at sea.'
LORD CARSON, Irish politician

Defining idea...

How did it go?

Q **I like the bit about working up a presentation because I've been told I'm quite good at them. Doesn't this idea mean having to check to see if they will have the necessary equipment to allow me to show my visual aids?**

A *Yes, it does and this is no bad thing. You'll have to ring them to ask. This displays keenness and preparation and puts you slightly ahead of the crowd. You'll probably find that they can accommodate you and may be intrigued to be asked. If they don't have the facility, you can always take a printout of your Powerpoint slides in big type and present them on the table, or show the slides from your laptop screen. By the way, don't go on too long.*

Q **I just missed out on a job. I was ready for the question put the way this idea puts it, but they actually asked, 'Why are you not earning more money at your age?' I floundered. What could I have done?**

A *This is a vice that you need to turn into a virtue. 'I've been concentrating on self-development and gaining the right kind of experience, on the grounds that if I do those things well the money will eventually come.'*

24

Give me an example in your career where you felt like giving up but managed to keep going

This question says, 'Are you hungry enough?' If you are, then you should look forward to this question in whatever guise it comes. You need a good story.

Show them the Rottweiler in you with a tale of grit and determination.

In most jobs there comes a time when it does seem too much. Normally there's a combination of factors that contribute to making your job almost too difficult. Don't hold back on this question; they really do want to make sure that when the chips are down they can rely on you to keep going.

IF YOU CAN KEEP YOUR HEAD...

The ingredients of the story are pretty straightforward. The circumstances have to be unpredictable; otherwise you should have seen the situation coming and taken avoiding action. It's quite good if someone else involved did give up and even better

Here's an idea for you...

Select some aspect of your job that's causing you some pain. Now analyse the situation and work out what would need to happen to improve the situation and take some grief off your shoulders. The solution will probably involve more resources of people, money or equipment. Work out what the benefits, preferably financial, would be to your organisation if more resources were invested. This exercise will help you to answer the obvious follow-up question: 'How did you build the plan that convinced your boss to put more resources in?' Be careful. Make sure that you show that you couldn't have got the same result by working smarter rather than investing more resources.

if there was an easy way that you could've got out of the situation without looking like a quitter.

'As a fairly raw salesperson I was sent to take over all the defence customers in Scotland as a specialist salesperson. The customers were in aerospace, missile technology and other quite high-profile and definitely high-spending areas of business. Frankly, I had underestimated just how much resentment there would be from the geographically based salespeople who'd looked after the accounts until then. I got through that and established a reasonable relationship with the whole sales force within about three months. I was heavily dependent, though, on the two main support staff who knew the customers well.

'Then four things happened at the same time. We brought out a new product range that all my customers wanted to know about. The Americans escalated their war in Asia, bringing huge new demands for deliveries from my customers and therefore from my company. The most senior support person moved jobs because he found the workload just too much, and I was asked to coordinate the impending two-day visit of the managing director. I had been working six and even seven days a week for long hours and my wife was telling me to call it a day and get a sensible job. When a big customer complained to my manager that he was not seeing enough of me, I definitely thought about chucking it in.

IDEA 41 looks at the other side of this with *Give me an example in your career where you felt like giving up and did.*

Try another idea…

'I decided against it. I rather tricked my boss into visiting a customer in Inverness with me. This gave me five hours of her time in the car going through some of the most wonderful scenery in the world. I finally convinced her to resource the plan I'd worked out that would get me back on track. I still worked very hard but quite quickly got on top of the job again. I'm really glad I didn't give up, partly because it's against my instincts and partly because, when all was said and done, I made a ton of money in bonuses that year.'

I'M ALL RIGHT; IT'S THE OTHERS

Another way of asking this question goes like this: 'Tell me about the most difficult situation you've found yourself in.' They may be looking to see if you'll fall into the trap of blaming other people. It tells them a lot if you talk about a situation where you got into a corner because of the incompetence of others. Always take responsibility for the situations you find yourself in.

'We shall not flag or fail…We shall fight on the beaches, we shall fight on the landing grounds, we shall fight in the fields and in the streets, we shall fight in the hills; we shall never surrender.'
WINSTON CHURCHILL

Defining idea…

105

How did it go?

Q **This gives me a problem. The main reason I am applying for this somewhat sideways move in the same organisation is that my current job is really getting to me and I desperately want to get into a position that's easier to manage. How do I handle this question in those circumstances?**

A *Tricky. Despite the advice above, in your situation you probably do need to blame someone else – your family. Don't show any sign of weakness. On the contrary, express very positive thoughts about the current job – 'I'm enjoying the challenge.' Make sure it doesn't look as though you're leaving behind a huge pile of poo for the next person to walk into – 'I've got the situation into a state where, with a thorough briefing from me, someone should be able to take over quite easily at this time.' And then hit them with, 'I want to spend more time with my family.'*

Q **Having done what you suggest and shown how I hung on in one situation, will it add to my credibility if I briefly describe another situation where I decided that the right choice for me was to admit defeat and get out of it entirely?**

A *No.*

25

Where have you made your organisation take a big risk?

This is a combination question. They're looking to make sure that you are a risk taker, and they're also checking that given a big idea you've got what it takes to drive it through even a sceptical organisation.

Companies make big growth jumps by taking risks. Senior people know this and are prepared to back good people if the return is high enough and the risk has been mitigated as far as possible.

Here's a template and example for answering this question along with the supplementary questions that interviewers will tend to ask. To find your optimal answer you'll need to include as many as possible of the principles here in a true story.

Here's an idea for you...

If you haven't been the leader of a project that took a serious risk, you could perhaps use experience from a risky project where you had even a fairly minor part. Talk to the project manager and see if you can develop the scenario from their point of view. Don't overplay your role; just explain what you learnt from being involved.

I RISKED WRECKING A KEY BRAND

You've got to show that you took a calculated risk after doing a careful analysis. Don't look reckless or whimsical. The question will come in a number of ways: 'Tell me about an idea that you've had to push hard to get accepted by your company.' 'In what circumstances have you shown initiative?' In most cases you should be able to start with the idea, explain why it was a risk, or a big risk, how you got it accepted by showing how well you'd mitigated the risk and what the result was.

'I was convinced that a brand we sold was doing much less than its potential because we were more or less marketing it exclusively to men. I worked on a campaign, TV and poster advertising, aimed at making the exact same product appeal to women. When I first presented it, many people wouldn't even hear me out. They pointed to first principles of marketing – that such a move might not only fail to attract the new market but also lose the loyalty of the original market. If men think they've been consuming a kind-of macho drink, how will they take to its being advertised to the opposite sex? I was ready for this and had done the research in both ways, testing to see if women would go for it, and also testing to see if the advertising would turn men off. I also proposed a small pilot market. Thus, given the absolutely staggering return if women changed their drinking habits, I had a good case. I needed heavyweight support, so had involved a very senior manager throughout and she certainly helped. Well, to cut a long story short, we did it, although with a number of people still adamantly opposed. And it was a huge success.'

YES, BUT WHAT ABOUT...

They'll probe on risk: 'Surely the small market pilot could've infected the larger market via newspaper articles or word of mouth?' 'I chose a fairly isolated market.' 'What was the fallback if the pilot had gone horribly wrong?' 'We could go back to positioning the product only for men and we were confident that this would work if we acted quickly.'

They'll probe on politics: 'The people who remained sceptical, did any of them see it as not in their interest for the project to succeed?' 'We really tried to get people to have at least an open mind, fearing that lukewarm support in some quarters could make things very difficult. I would say that there was a certain amount of armed neutrality. And, in the end if someone wants to climb out on a limb after the decision is taken, that's up to them.' This last shows a pretty forceful attitude to getting things done.

They may check you haven't burnt yourself out: 'It must have been very hard and stressful work. Would you do it again?' 'With what I've learnt from that exercise, I would handle another comparable situation very well and with a lower level of stress.'

There's more on being influential in IDEA 31, *What's the key to influencing people in parts of the organisation where you have no direct control?*

Try another idea...

'*Criticism is a life without risk.*'
JOHN LAHR, drama critic

Defining idea...

109

How did it go?

Q   **The riskiest decision I've made was followed by a less than 100% successful outcome. But I can answer all the questions you raise in this idea, particularly how we recovered the situation. It was a high risk, though. Could I use this example?**

A   *Frankly, it's not ideal; but if you came out of the situation smelling of roses and there's someone senior who would say that, it might work. If you do use it, emphasise how early you read the warning signs. The last thing you want is to give the impression it went pear shaped on you when you were still confident of success. It might be better to use another project where everything went well. It's a lower-risk option, if you see what we mean.*

Q   **My best example of this was with a company that had a rigid risk assessment system that really constrained what you could and couldn't do. If I explain all that, it'll look as though the system took the risk rather than me. Should I keep quiet about that?**

A   *Yes and no. It's a good idea to display your knowledge of such processes; so do tell them that you went through it all, and how much it taught you. But remember that processes depend on the input they receive. It was you who decided on the range of possibilities and on the most likely outcome. Call the process a good guideline to follow, but take full credit for taking the plunge.*

26

Do you feel your lack of financial knowledge will be a disadvantage?

You won't tick every box on their wish list; so you need to know the key ones. Think through what you think they will regard as essential attributes and use the interview to check them out.

Good interviewers will cover a broad range of topics. Researching or second-guessing the key ones helps you to hit the hot buttons and skate elegantly over the thinner ice.

Most companies, and probably all large companies, are well organised when they go recruiting. Their managers will have done their preparation aided by HR contacts and processes. They've agreed to talk to you, so it's unlikely that your CV has revealed a deal breaker. You'll have some knowledge of how important, say, financial knowledge is to this job from reading the advert carefully and asking for the job description before you go to the interview.

Here's an idea for you...

Make sure you're applying for the right jobs. If the same lack of knowledge or experience keeps stopping you getting jobs, you'll have to do something radical about it or work out an alternative route to getting where you want to be. It's never a good idea to keep banging your head against a brick wall. The best people to help you understand the real problem are those who've interviewed you and not selected you. Ask all of them for feedback in the specific area where they felt your knowledge and experience let you down. Talk to them about whether and how you could put it right.

IF THEY CAN DO IT, YOU CAN DO IT

First of all, know where the thin ice is. The chances are you already know where your weak areas lie for this job. But if you're uncertain what their priorities might be, use their own system to work it out. Make a table with three columns. In the left-hand column put down the knowledge and experience you think they will be looking for. Some will be straightforward, such as 'project management'; others softer, like 'motivating third parties'. Now anticipate their weighting of the importance of each of the capabilities you've identified, using a scale of 1–10, and write these in the second column. In the third column use a scale of 1–10 to record candidly your position right now. The best thing to do next is to check your opinion with someone who knows you and your work well. Now you should know what questions may be raised. How should you answer them?

TURNING A VICE INTO A VIRTUE

First, admit the weakness and show enthusiasm about fixing it. 'Yes, I know that's a bit of a crack in my armour, but it's one I want to put right and this job is a great opportunity to do that. My view is that I can do that in time to avoid any risk to achieving the goals of the job.' Their response to this will give you come clues as to whether there's a real problem or not. If they say, 'Yes, you're right,' you've not only answered the question but removed the obstacle. In any case make sure your answer exhibits 'good self-insight' here. At least you know your weaknesses.

> For a breakdown of leadership capabilities use IDEA 2, *What makes you a good leader?*

Try another idea...

Another way of handling this is to say that in the past you've found that often a new person in a team who does lack experience in one particular area may actually come up with a new angle that the team, used to operating in their usual way, might have missed.

Incidentally, if your weakness is in an area such as finance – a weakness mainly of knowledge – take heart. It's a lot easier to mug up such knowledge from a book than to earn the trust of your team or to manage difficult people. Point that out in the nicest possible way.

If they're still showing some concern it's a good idea to have already done something about the weak area. In this particular instance try, 'I knew that finance was a weak area so I took some advice from a financial controller on

> '*He had read Shakespeare and found him weak in chemistry.*'
> H. G. WELLS

Defining idea...

which book I should read. She suggested *Smart Things to Know about Business Finance* by Ken Langdon and Alan Bonham; so I bought it and I'm cracking on with it.'

Another useful technique here is the parallel answer – 'I haven't done that, but I have done this':

Them: Tell me about your experience in mergers and acquisitions.
You: I've not been directly involved with M&A; but I have handled complex projects where I had to rely on outside people for their particular expertise.

How did it go?

Q **OK, did the table and found it quite helpful, thanks. There is, however, one area where I think they're looking for '8' on the scale and I'm kind to myself if I mark myself '4'. Should I try to ignore this finding at the interview?**

A *Everyone's different, but we'd suggest you might bring this issue up early in the discussion. If you try to ignore it you might look nervous or not do yourself justice because you're sitting there hoping the topic will not be raised. Secondly, it's more impressive for you to have realised that you have this deficiency, and be prepared to do something about it, than to be found out by an awkward question.*

Q **There's a technical area in the job I'm applying for that they'll think is important but I happen to know is actually old hat and easily got round in other ways. What if I can't persuade them that they're out of date?**

A *It would be better not to try if you really think they're going to stick to their guns. Listen carefully to how they talk about the subject and ask questions about how receptive they would be to doing things another way. Then make a decision either to advocate the new technique or to abandon that tactic and use the weakness mitigation process instead.*

27

Is there anything you want to ask me?

This often comes near the end of the interview. If everything's gone well then make sure you don't at this point snatch defeat from the jaws of victory. On the other hand, if you think there's a problem, here's a good opportunity to go back into an area where you think they have doubts about you.

The worst answer here without any doubt is 'no.' It can look as though you're not much interested in the job, and it can indicate poor preparation.

By this time you ought to be having a sensible and interesting discussion with good rapport. So give two answers to this question: an open question that keeps the discussion going and a closed or more specific question that will elicit more insight into what it's like working for these people. After all, there are two decisions to be made here: they make the first decision, whether to offer you the job; then you have to decide whether to work for them.

You can strengthen most of the questions you want to ask by using your research. If, for example, you've read the recent press about the company you can ask the competition question much better. 'I understand your main competitor is X. Is that right and who do you feel are the main players making progress in the industry?'

MORE ABOUT THE INDUSTRY AND THEIR POSITION IN IT

Start by illustrating your preparation. Use something as up to date as possible. 'I'd like to hear a bit more about the industry and your position in it. There was an interesting piece in *The Times* about this Christmas being the worst for the retail industry for ten years, despite the fact that overall sales increased by 2.5%. Can you explain that and how do you see the next few years for retail generally?' You may think that question a bit too specific if, for example, you think they might struggle with the first bit. So go even more open. 'This industry has been very successful for a while now. How do you see it maintaining that progress?' This should get one or two of them going and you will listen and show that you're learning.

Another good area to probe around at this time is their competition. It's good to join an organisation that recognises it's in competition and that most companies in their industry have strengths and weaknesses. (Be careful here. Don't let yourself down by looking as though you know nothing about their industry. If you've prepared this question, don't ask it if the ground has already been covered.)

'Who do you regard as your main competition and who do you see becoming a bigger threat in the future?' It's a great idea to ask a question that's broader than the job itself. For example, if the job's in Europe, ask something about the worldwide performance or strategy. The point is to show your interest in the future as well as the present.

AND SPECIFICALLY...

Be careful. Silly as it may seem, this simple question has sunk more strong interviews than many more sinister-sounding salvoes. Don't focus too much on salary reviews, promotion prospects, type of car you get, parking spaces and so on. If there are important questions you want answers to, by all means ask them. Make sure, however, that you don't look as though these things are all that's important to you: ask some softer questions about the environment in which you'll be working. 'If you had to sum up in a few words the type of person who likes working here and the type of person who gets on well, what would they be?'

You can always turn a dual question back on them: 'What would you say are the main benefits of working for your organisation and the main frustrations?' 'Can I ask you if you have any reservations about my suitability for the job which we could discuss at this stage?' 'I am applying for other positions; but I'm particularly keen on this one. Is it possible to tell me when you'll make a decision?'

Final note: don't look as though your one and only reason for wanting to join them is to make money!

IDEA 14, *Why do you want to work for this company?* talks about the research you need to do before attending an interview.

Try another idea...

'*Holding hands at midnight*
'*Neath a starry sky,*
Nice work if you can get it,
And you can get it if you try.'
IRA GERSHWIN, US songwriter

Defining idea...

119

How did it go?

Q **This chapter emboldened me. It made me feel that in previous interviews I'd been too meek in questioning them about why I should go and work for them. So when they asked this question I simply said, 'Why should I come and work for you?' One person spluttered a bit and then went over some ground that we'd already covered. The other one said, 'Isn't that a bit of an arrogant question?' I backpedalled madly, saying that I hadn't meant to be arrogant and that maybe I'd phrased the question a bit wrongly. It was OK in the end, but I felt I'd given way when perhaps I shouldn't have. Anyway I got the job. What do you make of all that?**

A *You probably overstepped the line a touch by asking the question so brusquely. Always remember that they are in the driving seat because they're doing the hiring. Ask the same question with a softer touch: 'What would you say are the main reasons why people like working for your organisation?'*

Q **Listen, with the best will in the world I'm not going to read the Financial Times every day on the off-chance there will be something useful in it. What can I do instead?**

A *You can search the website of a financial newspaper or any investment website that tracks the performance of the company you're interested in. That way it'll take only a couple of minutes to find the latest published news about a company.*

28

Tell me of a time when you generated a creative solution to a problem

OK, they're looking for creativity and you've got to show them you've got it. Your example can be big or small. You don't need to have designed a brand new product; any change that you originated can be a good answer.

Always look for the benefits to your organisation and its customers.

Managers who succeed normally have creativity as a key attribute. Being 'creative' simply means having a good idea and implementing it. It's also about not accepting things as they are because, 'That's the way we've always done it.' So the quick answer to the question for most people has to be, 'Yes, I made something happen.'

THINK HARD AND USE OBSERVATION

Here are two examples, one where a fact of life seemed to limit the business that a small retail outlet could do, and the other an example of watching people's behaviour and coming up with a neat idea.

Here's an idea for you... **Look at the way you do your job from a customer's point of view. Look at all the processes involved. It's almost certain that something could be improved that you could suggest. Now sell your suggestion to your boss and you've made progress for your organisation and got a simple but good example of creativity for your next interview.**

'After I'd been the manager of the ladies' boutique for two months, I was thinking about the peaks and troughs that the business went through. It was quite simple. During the weekend we were very busy and had two extra people in. During the week we were fairly dead. But nevertheless we had to provide our service every day of the week. I started to think about what else we could use the premises for during the week. We served coffee; we stayed open at lunch. It seemed nothing more could be done. Then I saw the new fashion for nail parlours, and put two and two together. I did a deal with a nearby businesswoman who agreed to use our shop as a parlour two-and-a-half days a week. The combination of the two worked and we made a little money out of the nails service itself, but more importantly we raised clothes sales by 20%. We also think that we'll improve customer loyalty, since the customers who use the service love it: once someone is in the habit of getting their nails done regularly, we get a regular selling opportunity.'

Our second example features a good creative observer: 'I work in fashion accessories. My friend and I had been laughing at all the women rummaging around in their handbags when their mobile phones rang – and as often as not failing to get to it before it stopped ringing. I suggested to my company that we sew a special pocket into our top-range handbags to carry a phone. Women immediately saw the benefit of the simple feature. They even saw the financial benefit of not having to call everyone back all the time. The company saw an uplift in sales values as women traded up to the more expensive range.'

AND IT COULD BE YOU

You can be in any job you like and still be creative: 'I run the induction training for my company. Because of the nature of our business, health and safety takes up most of the training time. It struck me that new trainees were well versed in health and safety but knew almost nothing about our customers when they went into the field. I suggested we do something about this to my boss, and she thought it a good idea and asked me to come up with a plan. In the end I got one or two customers to come and talk to the trainees and answer questions. It worked very well. I've had very good feedback from the trainees. The customers I involved were very impressed, and staff were able to deal with customers from day one rather than handing them over to more experienced people. My boss thinks that this idea has played a part in improving sales.' So, it has got to be your initiative, it must be a fresh approach and there have to be benefits to company and customers.

An optimist is bound to be better at suggesting improvements than a pessimist. Have a look at IDEA 44, *Would you say you're a glass-half-empty person or a glass-half-full?*

Try another idea...

'You can't stop. Composing's not voluntary, you know. There's no choice, you're not free. You're landed with an idea and you have the responsibility to that idea.'
HARRISON BIRTWISTLE, British composer

Defining idea...

123

How did it go?

Q **I was asked, 'What problems occur in doing your job, and what are you doing about them?' I decided to take this as a creativity question and used a story in which I'd seen a problem at work and come up with an innovative solution. I told the truth, which involved saying that the idea had cost a bit of money but everyone had been delighted. I was a bit knocked back when the interviewer said, 'So you think it's worth changing things, even if it costs money off the bottom line to do it?' Why didn't it work for me?**

A *First of all, it was a good idea to take the question the way you did. This question can expose weakness when people talk about a problem without showing that they're doing something about it. Perhaps you didn't need to talk about the cost if you couldn't offer compensating benefits. Perhaps you could have made a stronger case for the benefits and only mentioned costs if asked.*

Q **My best example was an idea that looked as though it would be of huge benefit to the company; but circumstances changed and we abandoned it. It was a neat piece of lateral thinking. Can I use it?**

A *Probably the best way to use it is to precede it with a less spectacular innovation that yielded bottom-line results. Then you can talk more confidently about the big one.*

29

How important to you is your work/life balance?

The answer to this is important, as much to you as it is to them. Make sure you do know what that balance should be before you go in. Here's a way of working that out – plus some suggestions to make them love your answer.

There's no point in just being a safe pair of hands for the job. That just puts you up with the others. Add some flair and evidence to your answers and you'll stand out.

Everyone is going to say that they're indeed looking for a balance and that their partner/children/interests blah, blah, blah are important as well as their career. Here's a quick process that'll help you to know what you really want and at the same time give you an interesting way of answering the question.

WORK OUT YOUR STARTING POINT

There are 168 hours in the week, of which you spend 56 in bed. This leaves 112 for living in. Draw a three-by-three matrix of nine square boxes and write an activity

Here's an idea for you...

We're going to come across a number of questions where your research will be much improved if you have a friendly contact in the organisation you are interviewing for. This is one of them. Question them about the culture of the organisation and its attitude to work/life balance. It's very valuable to have that information before you go in.

heading in each of them. The headings will include some of the following: friends, relationships, family, alone time, personal development, health, hobbies, leisure, creativity, work and any other areas of life that you enjoy or endure. If you need more squares just add them. Don't forget to add areas in which at the moment you do nothing but which you wish to get involved in.

Now list the number of hours in a typical week you spend in each of these areas, convert it to a percentage of 112 and write the percentage in the appropriate box.

That's your starting point. You may wish to check what you have written with your partner and a work colleague to make sure you're not indulging in wishful thinking. If the percentages are just what you want, well done; you just have to think through how to tell the interviewer this.

One person who did this exercise decided that he was spending too many hours watching television and too many hours working. The box that suffered from this was the one marked 'wife and family'. He resolved therefore to switch the TV off between Monday and Thursday. He told his boss he was only going to work late three evenings a week and that he was leaving each Wednesday and Friday at five o'clock. He started to take his wife out for dinner once a month and told his two sons that every other weekend they could have half a day of his time to do anything they wanted to do provided it didn't cost more than twenty dollars. He actually implemented a plan that was OK with his boss and delightful for his family.

There's more on this subject in IDEA 12, *How ambitious are you?*

Try another idea...

PLAN THE SITUATION FOR THE FUTURE

Now look at the areas where you want to make adjustments. For every area whose percentage you increase you have to make a choice about which area you are going to reduce. Add in any activities that currently you don't do but have resolved to get started on. Now convert the percentages into hours and see if you believe you have a feasible plan.

That's the exercise. Now turn it into a brilliant answer to the question. It's probably a good idea to suggest you've gone through such a process. Tell them what the answer is. Watch their faces, though; some of them may be workaholics and think that's the only way for an ambitious person to be. Add a safety-first rider like, 'I think that when anyone starts a new job they probably have to work a lot of hours to get it under control; if necessary during that time I'll work all the hours God sends.' You can also point out that people who achieve a good work/life balance tend to be more effective at work. It's not just the hours you work; it's your attitude to getting things done.

'It is impossible to enjoy idling thoroughly unless one has plenty of work to do.'
JEROME K. JEROME, British essayist

Defining idea...

How did it go?

Q **I'm trying to change my work/life balance away from work. That's why I'm applying for this new job. I'd like to work less than forty hours per week – thirty-five if possible. Is this an acceptable reply?**

A *It has to be really. If they don't know and appoint you, then either or both of you are going to be disappointed. Careful how you word it, though. You're trying to look like a person who makes a good contribution at work but has other important things to do, not a work-shy skiver.*

Q **I'm trying to get a promotion in a company I already work for. The team I'm trying to join are in the habit of going for a drink after work most days. Quite honestly, I don't fancy that and would prefer to use that time in other ways. Should I tell them?**

A *Ah, no. When you join you'll find it easy enough to join them from time to time without its becoming an uncomfortable habit. We would put this time firmly in the work part of the matrix, join them to keep up with the internal politics and slip out when it becomes idle chatter. But there's no need to explain all that in the interview.*

30

What really gets you up in the morning looking forward to work?

Your response here reveals a lot about you. Think about the main points you're trying to make about you and this job. Show how you've spent time and energy in creating what for you is an ideal working environment.

Answer with a big smile, look as though you're enjoying answering this question and perhaps indicate that it's a lot of things in combination that add up to a happy working life.

Companies, particularly their HR function, know that people who come to work with enthusiasm spread their enthusiasm to other people. They also know that performance is much improved where people enjoy the time they're at work. So they're looking for the kind of person who generates such an ambience.

Here's an idea for you...

This is a very good question to role-play as practice with a friend or colleague. Role-play is a powerful tool for preparation work. It's extraordinary how much easier it is to field a question if you've tried it out the previous day. When you prepare an answer in your head, you tend to leave loose ends that you might not be entirely sure how to finish off in real life. Role-play forces you to face these and tie them off. It's brilliant if you can find someone who knows the interviewer to enact their part.

LOOK FOR A FOCUS

Consider how your skills, training and experience focus upon this job. Let's imagine that the interviewers are looking mainly for a good team leader, someone with good customer relationship skills as well as a professional technician. The answer comes out a bit like this: 'First and foremost nowadays, I'd say it's the team. We're working well together now. We lost the one person who I felt was holding us back from making the team something much bigger than the sum of the parts. Since then morale has just climbed. The feedback I'm getting on their pride in being in the team is terrific. I'm even getting it from people in other teams who have noticed the change.'

That answer would probably lead to the question: 'You sound as though you turned this team round. How did you do it?' 'Using quite a simple activity really. When I arrived, people felt as though they had no part in any decision-making process. There was no formal way of consulting them and they didn't feel it was part of their job to knock on a door and make a suggestion. I used the "bacon roll technique" I'd learnt from a great team leader I'd worked for. Every Monday morning at 8.15 a.m. I brought a bacon roll into the office for everyone in the team – engineers, admin, secretaries, the lot. They knew it was going to happen so they all started to be there in time. For half an hour we discussed items on a short agenda and then for the last fifteen minutes we took any other business. Believe me, that could go anywhere. That was the start. People started to feel a sense of pride in being part of the team.'

Another version of this is found at IDEA 20, *In your current role what are you most proud of achieving?*

Try another idea...

Another good answer about your motivation: 'I'm really energised when I know that what I'm doing is making a real difference.'

YOU CAN FACE OUTWARDS AND STILL BE METICULOUS

'Another thing that I really enjoy is the customer-facing part of the job. I enjoy meeting customers and they sure do their bit to make our lives interesting. There's always something new to think about and new people to deal with. Finally, I'm motivated by the complex project side of things. We're at the leading edge with a number of our customers and we have to make some very complicated decisions and come up with innovative ways of solving problems. I've always liked that.'

Expect a supplementary question on that last bit: 'Are you still heavily involved in the technical details of the projects in your area?' To which you might answer, 'I try not to be. I've got an excellent team who can handle that side of things. We have a standing joke that my product knowledge is sketchy and they tease me that I'm out of date. I still get my hands dirty from time to time, though, and I think they know that if I have to get into the detail I can still do it.'

'Awake, my soul, and with the sun
Thy daily stage of duty run.
Shake off dull sloth, and joyful rise,
To pay thy morning sacrifice.'
THOMAS KEN, British divine

Defining idea...

How did
it go?

Q **I tried role-play with an old mate. It didn't really work. To begin with I felt nervous and under pressure. Then it just didn't feel real. I'm sure I'd have done better in real life than in the role-play. I'm not going to do it again because I think it might lower my confidence. Do you think that's the right decision for me?**

A *You're absolutely right to say that you'll be better in real life than in the practice. That's always the case: ask an actor. The point is that the practice makes you concentrate on the content of your answers and get some feedback. Now you've got over the worst of the nervousness try the same role-play again and we bet you anything you do it better.*

Q **I'm a salesperson and they're always trying to make me role-play although I keep telling them that I'm no good at role-play. They catch me out saying things I wouldn't actually say to a real customer. Isn't it too artificial an environment?**

A *Our experience is the opposite of what you've just said. People do say to customers what they say in role-play; it's just that most customers are too polite to point out the mistakes that employees make. We've found a huge correlation between a successful performance in role-play and successful performance in real life. If you're still reluctant to do it, you can get some of the benefit by role-playing both sides yourself, as long as you articulate both parts aloud.*

31

What's the key to influencing people in parts of the organisation where you have no direct control?

In today's organisations cross-functional teams and cross-discipline projects are becoming more and more necessary. Give an answer that demonstrates that you understand the need and have thought about how to respond to it.

The whole organisation should be geared towards excellent customer service. This involves talking to people outside your department and getting all the departments to work together.

Not only talking to them but also steering them towards your way of thinking if that's best for the organisation. One of the places where processes such as, say, customer service go wrong most often is when the process moves from one department to another. These events are sometimes known as 'stand-offs'.

Here's an idea for you...

For the job you're applying for compose a list of 'stakeholders' – people, from senior to very junior, who are in some way involved with the quality of how you will get the job done. List also the departments where you will have an interface and whose help you're going to need from time to time. This will give you a very solid base for the answer to a question like this.

IT'S GOT TO BE GENUINE AND OPEN

Start from the need, go on to how people can get it wrong and then explain exactly how to influence people you do not directly control: 'Yes, I've heard it called "inspirational leadership" and that's a good term. You have to get someone to want to help and be adaptable to your requirements. It definitely doesn't work if people realise that they never hear from you unless you want them to do something. What we do is this. We have a list of all the people whose teams and work affect us either all the time or from time to time. We divide them up among us and take actions to keep in touch with them frequently and continually. We try to show a genuine interest in what they do and to understand as well as we can how they work. Then when the time comes when we want to influence how they do their job we have that relationship as a start. It works quite well. I also try to be a net exporter of favours – I like to have done a few things for other people, so that when I need something in return I've already shown willing. "You scratch my back and I'll scratch yours" may not be in the textbooks but it's worked from the beginning of time.'

'That's a good answer; but why do you think all organisations have inter-departmental blind spots?' Explain, 'I think it's quite simple: people don't get out of their environment enough and visit their colleagues. Hewlett Packard call it "managing by wandering around" – and that's a great concept.'

Inspirational leadership is a lot to do with passion. If you passionately want to provide a top-quality service then others around you will catch that bug. The opposite is certainly true. If you're not passionate about doing your job to the best possible standard, you sure as hell can't expect anyone else to be.

Another example of influencing people is in IDEA 49, *The division you'd be managing has its head right down at the moment: how will you set about re-motivating them?*

Try another idea...

SOMETIMES YOU HAVE TO USE THE SANDBAGS

Such sweetness and light don't always work, however. 'Just suppose for a moment that the manager in another department is completely intransigent. They just won't give an inch towards your need for them to change the interface between the two of you. What do you do then?'

Don't hold back. Use either your own experience or the experience of a colleague: 'Actually, this has happened to me. A supervisor in credit control would not make a slight adjustment to his system that we needed. He could've made it easier for us to give out information to customers from one desk, rather than passing them over to another person. I learnt two things from this situation. One was how not to do it: I went to the supervisor's boss direct, she supported her team member and the relationship between him and me got even worse. I really think I'd tried everything but in this case had to resort to escalation. I took the case up the line until I got to the board director who controlled both departments. She looked at the situation, realised that credit control were being unreasonable and crashed down on them, insisting that they make the change.'

'A teacher affects eternity; he can never tell where his influence stops.'
HENRY BROOKS ADAMS, US historian

Defining idea...

How did it go?

Q **I'm going for a promotion in a division where such cross-functional reciprocity just doesn't exist. The division is highly process driven and if you want someone to do something differently you have to go through the huge grief of getting an inter-departmental process changed. The head of the division will be at the interview. Do you think I should answer a question in this area by saying we ought to lighten up the bureaucratic burden and talk to each other more?**

A *Yes, but with great care. Try to use an example where you broke down a barrier and with another person in a different function got something done quickly. From there you might talk about the frustration that other people are feeling about being hog-tied by process. It makes a neat point: you're not frustrated – you just get on with it and achieve results – but others are.*

Q **I lost a job the other day because one of the interviewers was amazed that I didn't have 'process maps' that showed the workflow of everything we do and how things travel from one department to another. Is she right? Should I have been able to demonstrate such process maps? If so, where can I find out about them?**

A *Yes, they're right. For an organisation that's really trying to improve continuously and learn all the time, process maps are part of the base information it needs. Try* Strategic Thinking *by Andy Bruce and Ken Langdon.*

32

May I pass you over now to my colleague?

Aha, you're in a panel interview. There are special techniques for handling a group of people in a more formal environment.

The difficulty in panels is maintaining the interest of all the members at all times.

As an example of panel interviews, we'll take a type that many organisations use. They put a hurdle in place that all potential managers from all parts of the business must jump if they are to move into management at all. This is not an interview for a specific job, but a check to ensure that you have what it takes to make the first rung of the corporate ladder. You need to pass such panels first time and preferably easily and unanimously.

KEEP EVERYBODY INTERESTED

The panel interview is a more formal process and less of a conversation. Prepare thoroughly and try to be precise in your answers rather than more conversational. Use questions to establish quickly the role of each panel member. Try to make all the members of the panel speak, and then listen to what they say. All the clues will

Here's an idea for you... **As part of your preparation speak to a wider section of people than just your boss. The latter will be helpful, true, but their experience of these matters could be out of date. You'll gain more from speaking to people who've recently passed a panel and, if you can find one willing to help, someone who's recently failed. Make sure that in the interview you display the preparation you have done; that puts you ahead of the crowd.**

be there. The HR person will know when in interviews it's right to hold their tongue, but the line managers will often respond, particularly if they have already listened to a number of enthusiastic talkers who listen very little.

Let's look at possible pitfalls. 'How will you go about the technical side of a project?' This one could take you into your comfort zone and make you go into too much detail. It's always possible to check that you're at the right level: 'Is this answering your question or do you want more detail?' should get an honest response from the chairperson. If you're answering a technical question that one panel member is interested in, still check on the others: 'I'm conscious that I'm going into some detail on this. Is that OK?'

'Why do you think this is the right time for you to go into management?' Square away your current job, and then show your ambition: 'We're coming to the end of the second phase of my current project; so it's good timing from my boss's point of view. Rather than moving on to another project, I feel that I'm ready to go up a gear. I think I've shown that I'm at my best when I'm given more and more responsibility and that's what I'm looking for in my next job.'

They're almost certain to ask about poor performers, since managers have to deal with some tough situations: 'What would you do if one of your team members was really not performing?' You need to show you have the authority to handle such a situation, but don't jump in with, 'Well, sack them.' Know the rules and procedures for what has to be done. Your answer needs to show them that when you've exhausted coaching,

There's more on not boring panel members in IDEA 5, *Talk me briefly through your history.*

Try another idea...

training and all the HR procedures, you will have the assertiveness to do what needs to be done and move the poor performer on if it's necessary. 'In the end it's not just me and the team who are in a bad situation; it's also the poor performer. It's in their interests as well to resolve the problem once and for all.'

REMEMBER YOUR BODY LANGUAGE

How do you keep in with everyone? First and foremost is eye contact. Keep it flowing across the whole panel all the time. It keeps everyone involved in the conversation and gives you the chance to pick up on their reactions. It's very tempting to limit your eye contact to the person who asked the question you're answering, or, probably worse, to speak almost exclusively to the senior person in the room. And there's a sex trap here. Some men dodge eye contact with the women on the panel and concentrate on the men. Nothing can be more guaranteed to make a female manager seethe, and quite right too: it's bloody rude. And it works the other way too. Some women interviewees keep more eye contact with women panel members. The men may take this as a sign of weakness – you're obviously looking for feminine support.

Defining idea...

'The function that distinguishes the manager above all others is their educational one. The one contribution they are uniquely expected to make is to give others vision and ability to perform. It is vision and more responsibility that, in the final analysis, define the manager.'
PETER DRUCKER, management consultant

141

How did it go?

Q **I really think that my husband's support allows me to work more effectively and without stress. Do you think it's a good idea for me to include my stable home environment among my strengths?**

A *Probably, but be careful to whom you're talking. I know someone who used this line to a panel that included a woman on her third husband, a man who had recently replaced his wife with his secretary and a manager whose messy divorce was still getting the occasional mention in the News of the World. It was a good story, just the wrong audience.*

Q **I've been told that panels like to hear that you've read some management books and are aware of some of the latest management techniques. Is this true?**

A *It can be, yes. Try to offer a sentence in this area. Don't be too clever. Some of the panel members may not know what you're talking about – in which case they may resort to dismissing it as 'management-speak' and not practical. In this regard 'holistic' is dangerous and 'e-synchronous supply chain' only for those who can explain it simply with references to examples from their organisation.*

33

Tell me about yourself

This is an open question that can go anywhere. You have to ask a clarifying question to make sure that you talk about the angle they're looking for.

Keep your answer succinct and ask frequently if you're covering the areas they want you to.

They may ask this question to open the interview, because it can expose under-preparation. The first thing to do is ask whether they want to hear about you the person or you in the context of your work. We'll take the former line and assume they answer with a question like, 'Take you the person first; what are you like?'

WHAT I LIKE ABOUT LIFE

This question allows you to use some well-prepared words and to try to settle in after a nervous start. (They don't want someone who's just as stressed at the end of the interview as they were at the beginning.) You should plan also to ask open questions in return so that your response develops into a conversation.

Probably the best structure for this centres on what you like and don't like. Match this approach to the personal attributes you think they're looking for. If the job

Here's an idea for you...

When you've decided what to say about yourself, talk it over with someone who knows you well. Remind them they've got to say what they really think or they could be doing more harm than good. Look up the results of any aptitude, personality or other tests you've done. Try to be consistent with what these told you about yourself. Such results also add credibility to the answers you give.

specification includes the terms 'innovation' and 'customer-facing skills' you might try something like, 'My starting point would be to say that I like solving problems. From my youngest days with Lego, when I preferred to design as well as build the models I made, to my passion for crosswords to the new challenge of bringing up children, I like to work out how to do things I've never done before. I'm not so happy when I have to go through routines there's no real possibility of changing. My husband points out that I can spend hours going through a car boot sale to find pictures and books, but that I seem reluctant to spend a shorter amount of time doing the weekly supermarket shop.'

Don't forget that they'll probe for the weakness in such a reply: 'Does this mean that you let the chores of work, like the administration and documentation, get behind?' Answer this in a reassuring way: 'I know the importance of keeping my admin up to date and I always ensure that I'm on top of it.'

Defining idea...

'Personal relationships are the thing for ever and ever, and not this outer life of telegrams and anger.'
E. M. FORSTER

An alternative gambit might be, 'I enjoy meeting new people. I'm sometimes a little nervous when I go into a situation where I'm with a lot of people I don't know, but I get over it fast. I often find myself being the one who introduces people and brings new people into conversations. I can stand my own company for a while, but I'm a very social animal.'

NATURE VERSUS NURTURE

The more work-oriented version of this question is covered in **IDEA 5, *Talk me briefly through your history.***

Try another idea...

To get to know you more deeply, the interviewer may ask, 'Do you think there are born salespeople/leaders/managers, or do you believe that you can train anyone to do these jobs?' Just hit the balance: 'It's a bit of both really. If you take very naturally to selling, it's important to remember that there's still a lot to learn. No one's born knowing the theory and practice of sales technique, but some people are better at implementing the theory once they've been taught it.'

'Some people do seem to be naturally inclined to be leaders in any given situation. But there's a lot more to it than that. The skills involved in leadership need to be learnt and practised. I really believe the old cliché when it comes to leadership: "You're never too old to learn."'

'The meeting of two personalities is like the contact of two chemical substances: if there is a reaction, both are transformed.'
CARL JUNG

Defining idea...

Q   At my last interview I kept tripping up on questions like this. Whatever I said, and however I proved the benefit of that personality trait, she would always ask a question about the downside of it. I found myself continuously on the back foot. How should I have tackled that?

How did it go?

A   *This is not all bad. Interviewers want to test your resilience to assertive questioning and this is a good way for them to do it. It's not too important if you get a bit tongue-tied – unless you haven't thought out what the downside might be. Try next time to pre-empt in your answer at least half of the supplementary downside questions.*

Q **I talked about my drive and energy, as well as how outgoing a person I am. I slowly realised that I was describing a person exactly the opposite of the person who was interviewing me. I battled on regardless. Was that the right thing to do?**

A *Not entirely. You needed to switch some of your answer to compliment the interviewer on their personal attributes. Emphasise your contemplative side and assure them of your great respect for thinkers and planners. It's just social skill really, to reflect your personality in a way that suits the person who's listening.*

Q **In a conversation in this area, she suddenly asked about my personal interests outside work. My instinct was that it was none of her business, and I answered the question badly. Do I have to answer this question?**

A *'Fraid so. The question may elicit some useful information about you. Give a straight answer but try to incorporate some benefit to the work context. 'I help with an extra reading class for children on Saturdays. It's certainly taught me patience and tolerance; and I love doing it.'*

34

In your current role what has been your major disappointment?

You have to be prepared to talk about some things that didn't go so well. The key here is to show what you learnt from the situation and how you would handle a similar situation better in the future.

Nobody's perfect. Don't lose confidence in answering this one. Lay your disappointment out quite openly. They're looking for honesty — and your attitude to risk.

This is a question from an experienced interviewer. They've used the word 'disappointment' and that's very helpful. In your answer you should stick with that sort of word and avoid words like 'failure' or 'loss'.

Here's an idea for you... **When something goes wrong there's normally a customer involved. They may be an external customer or an internal department to whom you provide a service. To prepare for this question go back to that customer and ask some open questions about what happened. This has two benefits. One is that they may well give you a better answer to the question than the one you had in mind. Secondly the interviewer's going to be impressed by, 'I went back recently to the customer to ask for more feedback now that the dust has settled.'**

I CANNOT TELL A LIE, IT WAS I WHO CUT DOWN THE TREE

Like George Washington you mustn't duck responsibility for the disappointment, even if you've got a cast iron excuse that what went wrong wasn't your fault. It's a bad worker who blames their tools, and a poor salesperson who blames the product or the company or anything else for not delivering the goods.

'I was disappointed when the effort we put into the big Bradford sales campaign didn't result in any more business than we were doing beforehand. We knew at the time that it was a risky use of our resources; but the reward we were shooting for seemed worth it and I really wanted to have a go. The team was raring to go as well. In terms of risk, the upside was huge and the downside disappointing, as opposed to disastrous – we were already pretty much on the annual target and any gain would have been the icing on the cake.'

'OK, so what went wrong?' Time to spill the beans using words like 'under-estimated' or 'miscalculated'. Emphasise that it's much easier to know what should have been done after the event: 'With the benefit of twenty-twenty hindsight, I probably misunderstood how important a client they were to the competition. I mean, no one likes losing business; but they poured effort and resource into keeping their share of the market. They lowered their price more than we had expected. In my preparation I'd warned the company what discount we would have to offer to get the business. If I'd done the calculation on an even bigger discount, I might have seen the campaign was not worth the effort.'

There's a question on declining risk in IDEA 6, *Tell me of a time when you were risk averse.*

Try another idea...

IT WON'T HAPPEN AGAIN

Move on now to what you've learnt from the situation; try to get in first rather than waiting for the question, 'So, what would you do differently next time?' Start with a process change that you would make and then something to do with people:

'The first thing I would do going into such a situation again would be to sit down with the customer and ask some hard questions about whether they are willing to consider changing their supplier. I'd get the project manager to proclaim this willingness in front of two senior

'Victory has a hundred fathers, but defeat is an orphan.'
COUNT GALEAZZO CIANO, Italian politician

Defining idea...

managers, one from their company and one from mine. That ought to help with commitment. The other thing I'd do is keep the team gung-ho about tackling the opportunity, but somehow warn them that there has to be a risk that it won't all go exactly as we would like. That way it would be less of a challenge to pick them up again after the event.'

Now, if you can add an insight for the whole company to learn from your experience, you've turned a potential snake into a good long ladder: 'I also think we might coordinate our resources when trying a big competitive battle like this. It would have been great if we'd looked as though we were threatening some other competitive accounts in the same area at the same time. That way the competition wouldn't have been able to concentrate so much resource against us.'

How did it go?

Q **I tried this out by ending with a positive. The interviewer then said that because of the positive statement he didn't think it was much of a disappointment and asked me for another example. What should I have done then?**

A *First of all, assure them that it was indeed a disappointment: 'Well, I was very disappointed. We tried to make the best of it, but it hadn't gone well.' Then you just have to give them another one. Perhaps before you give the positive at the end of the story you should again express your disappointment. That might prevent them asking for another.*

Q **I decided to be honest and told them about my greatest booboo. I once sacked someone but got some of the procedures wrong. The employee took us to a tribunal and it cost the company £50,000. I didn't get the job. What went wrong?**

A *It's not entirely surprising you didn't get the job. That result is not unconnected, we suspect, with your telling this story. Look, there's honesty and honesty; you don't have to tell them things like that unless they ask. Think of another disappointment and don't make it quite such a disaster. In the end remember that at all times in the interview you're selling yourself.*

35

Would you be surprised if I told you that my colleague found you a bit arrogant?

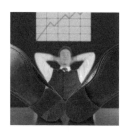

A question like this means that you haven't left someone with the impression you'd planned. Make sure you're acutely aware of the outcome you're aiming at and you're more likely to succeed. Take the remark positively.

It could be their colleague or it could, of course, be the speaker who's gained that impression. It's a mistake to go too defensive here.

Whether they are right or not, it's their prerogative to make a judgement on you. The question is as much aimed at testing your reaction to criticism as it is at the actual accusation.

Here's an idea for you...

Before you go into an interview write down exactly the impression you want to leave behind. It's like writing down a measurable objective: it helps to focus everything you do on the outcome you had in mind. So, if you think it's right to look confident, write that down. The same for professional, cheerful, easy to manage and so on.

FIND OUT HOW TO PUT THINGS RIGHT

It is perfectly fair in these circumstances to ask clarifying questions as well as try to explain what went wrong. 'Wow, that's really good feedback! Yes, I am a bit surprised because I don't think anyone's said that before. Is there anything in particular that gave them that impression?' This may give you a sounder basis for your explanation: 'I think I might have been trying too hard. I was determined to show a lot of confidence in my ability to do the job; maybe that shaded into my looking arrogant. The last thing I want is to be overbearing; that's not my style at all.'

Now see if you can connect this to other feedback that you have had and show how you went about correcting the fault: 'I have had feedback in the past that when I get a bit nervous I tend to overcompensate by displaying confidence quite assertively; but I try to bear that in mind when I'm under pressure.'

Other ways for the interviewer to get into this area include, 'How would you react if I told you that your presentation this morning didn't go down well?' The word 'if' is important here. They're not necessarily saying that it was poor. They want to know how you would react. Use the same confident template as above: 'First of all I'd thank you for the feedback. It's terribly important for me to learn from other people's opinions of me. Then I'd ask you to give me some more detail: was it the content or my

Defining idea...

'People ask you for criticism, but they only want praise.'
W. SOMERSET MAUGHAM

delivery that gave you a problem? Then I'd think about it and try to make sure that it didn't happen again.'

Think about a challenge to your knowledge: 'You don't seem to know much about our company.' Being told you're out of date: 'We thought we'd hear more of the modern methods of training, not just classroom courses.' Being challenged about your attitude: 'You don't sound as though you get up in the morning with a spring in your step as you think about your work.' Handle them all in the same way.

IDEA 7, *What are you like at getting difficult people to do things differently?* puts you on the other side of the criticism problem.

Try another idea...

WHAT'S THIS ONE ALL ABOUT?

When they're interviewing, everyone wants to make a judgement as to how easy it'll be to manage the person they're thinking of hiring. It's quite difficult to manage and develop someone who finds it impossible to receive criticism without taking it all personally and defending themselves vigorously. You have to spend a lot of time getting them to admit that something's wrong before the two of you can move on to putting it right. You don't have to have a hide like a rhinoceros nowadays, but it doesn't do to look thin-skinned either.

So your attitude in answering this question is as important as what you say. You must show that you recognise the duty of a manager to give feedback and occasionally criticism to their team. They want you to take it in a professional, objective and mature fashion.

'I am bound by my own definition of criticism: a disinterested endeavour to learn and propagate the best that is known and thought in the world.'
MATTHEW ARNOLD

Defining idea...

153

How did it go?

Q **I got a question like this about my part in a group role-play where I'd been trying to shut one of the people up who kept going on and on. The interviewer questioned my teamwork. I thought it rather unfair, but I did as you suggest and thanked them for the feedback and so on. When I'd finished he told me that I could have been more assertive in defending my position. What did I do wrong, or have you given me bad advice?**

A *It doesn't sound as though you did anything wrong; perhaps he was just pushing the topic 'taking criticism' another step further to see how you would react to his follow-up. It is, however, possible to look over-accommodating to a manager. No one wants a doormat in the team. The trick is to look easy to manage but capable of giving the odd surprise; after all, geniuses make their own rules. Anyway thank you for your feedback on our advice. We'll take it very seriously, and possibly reword it.*

Q **The appraiser asked me to comment on what she called areas where I needed to develop or improve. I argued against every single one and thought I'd successfully showed her that my conduct had been more or less faultless. If I'd read this Idea first I think I'd have accepted what she was saying and discussed her criticism more positively. As it was, she then went further down the list and marked me as unsatisfactory on 'taking criticism'. Not much I could say about that, was there?**

A *Bad luck. It's a good reminder that interviewers, like appraisers, have an awful lot of cards in their hand. That's why you have to think so hard about your interview technique.*

36

What's your style of influencing people?

This is a slightly trick question. The good team leader can change their style of influencing to suit the person they're working with.

You're likely to have a core style. Illustrate that and then illustrate how you can change it when necessary.

There's another angle to this question, like the Russian doll within the Russian doll. When you're in an interview, you are at that time trying to influence the interviewer. So make sure that the way you present the answer to this question reflects the demeanour and behaviour of the person you're addressing.

IT'S WHAT YOU SAY

Tell them outright why no single style will do for everyone: 'The main thing I've learnt about influencing people is that they're all subtly different and, though most people have a natural style, everyone has to fit horses to courses. I naturally have a consultative style, influencing people by discussion and joint planning. But it comes

Another angle upon this question concerns learning styles. Some people learn by jumping in at the deep end and doing something; others prefer to reflect long and hard before they act. Some people look very pragmatically at what works and doesn't work, while others want to understand all the theory behind what they're learning. Look around and think about the learning style of the people you work with. You could get some useful insights into how to manage them and a strong answer to questions about management style. There's lots of material on this: just search the web for 'learning styles'.

out differently for different people. For example, my influence over one member of my team consists almost entirely of listening to her as she works out what needs to be done and how to do it. With another person I find I have to spell things out much more, making suggestions and giving advice. Then there's another person who's very process oriented. I motivate and influence him by facilitating a decision-making or other business process.'

A bit of theory might come in handy: 'A lot depends on the circumstances as well. Some people talk about "push and pull" management styles; "push" being the "Do what you are told" or autocratic method, "pull" the consulting democratic way of leading people. I naturally lean towards pull, but when the chips are down I can switch into being more directive if events demand it.'

Then look at why people do things: 'I always try to remember that people work for money but do a bit extra for recognition, praise and reward. If I think someone is doing a good job I never forget to tell them. I show appreciation often. I find it best not to wait for the end of a task to say thanks. I don't find this too difficult. I'm genuinely interested in how people tick and can normally work out how to get the best out of them.'

What about creativity: 'Sometimes I like to hold back from influencing the team about a decision they're making. If I'm too involved in getting them to do what I think is best, I run the risk of stifling their creativity. If I let them get on with it, they do come up with the most amazing insights.'

Working with your boss is covered in IDEA 19, What's your definition of the ideal relationship with your boss?

Try another idea...

AND HOW YOU SAY IT

We've said that you're trying to influence the person on the other side of the desk. You have very little time to make up your mind how to do it. Some of it is quite obvious. If they behave rather formally, going dryly through a logical process and asking clipped questions, it's plainly inappropriate to slouch, crack jokes or comment widely outside the answer to the question. If the person is very informal you can be more relaxed and converse with them on their terms. (Don't go too far; you're trying to look like a professional businessperson not a stand-up comic.)

It's obviously much easier to get the formal/informal balance right if you've found out about the person before the start of the interview. In all cases it's hugely important to smile, thank them for what they say and do, thank them for good questions and use their name a lot in your responses.

Defining idea...

'When Brearley the England Captain felt that he needed to ginger Botham up, he would signal to me to do some stirring. I had to go up to Botham with a message – "Mike says that you're bowling like a girl." I'd then almost pity the poor batsman who faced the next ball from a seething Botham. If he'd used the same words with me it would have destroyed me, and Brearley, of course, knew that.'
BOB WILLIS, British cricketer

How did it go?

Q **My natural style is very low key and consultative. I'm going for an interview with a bloke who makes Genghis Khan look like a counselling therapist. He is highly autocratic, to say the least. Should I say what I feel, or say that I'm more directive than I really am?**

A *A bit of both, really. Your low-key and consultative answer will still work, but you need to put a bit more emphasis on your ability to get people to take direction. Take as an example a situation where you had to take control fast, like a fire or a furious customer. Remember that the guy might actually want someone with a very different style from his own. You never know.*

Q **I had two people in the interview, one very stiff and formal and the other rather slovenly and very friendly. Should I have treated them differently?**

A *Yes, it's quite possible to alter how you answer a question according to who asked it. But it's probably safer to err on the formal side. The more relaxed person is more likely to understand that you're doing it to stay onside with Mr Formality. Mr Formality may take against you if you're too friendly with the other person.*

37

What are your outside interests?

This may be a very important question for someone applying for their first job. The key is to find some connection between your interests and the job without sounding simplistic.

When looking at your outside interests, they're looking for where you've taken leadership whatever you were doing.

Watch out for someone who's as expert as or more expert than you in the leisure pursuit you're discussing. If you say you're passionate about opera, be prepared to go into some detail. An opera buff on the other side of the desk will certainly probe the depth of your passion. This is an important area to tell the truth. Don't exaggerate your knowledge or experience.

HOW HAS IT DEVELOPED YOUR EMPLOYABILITY?

Learning and leadership are the two main areas that outside interests can contribute to your being an effective employee. So don't just say what you do in your leisure time; relate it to one of these: 'I'm very interested in current affairs and

Here's an idea for you... **Surveys have shown a correlation between success in business and interest in sports; so if you haven't got involved yet, think about doing something, especially if you're a graduate looking for your first job. At least go out for a walk everyday. You might be able to make something out of that.**

indeed in most parts of the daily papers. At college I wrote an occasional news column in the student newspaper. In fact, for a while I was involved in the production of the paper. I never edited it but I used to do copy-editing and proofreading. I learnt a lot about how a bright bunch of people go about a shared task. It was sometimes pretty chaotic, but towards print day you could see the editor getting on top of it; and we always got it on to the streets at the right time. I gave it up in my final year; I was worried that it would take up too much time.' This last sentence is good because it explains in a responsible way why you didn't become editor.

Expect a lot of follow-up questions to an answer like that. 'What papers do you read?' If you only read a quality paper occasionally, it can be dangerous to claim knowledge of it; it may be the one the interviewer has been reading for twenty years. (If you only read tabloids, don't use this answer.)

The interviewers may refer back to your experience: 'What are the attributes of a good copy-editor?' Tell them: 'Good powers of concentration, good spelling and grammar and an interest in a wide range of topics.' 'What was it about the editor that helped them to pull things together?' Tell them: 'One in particular used to be very good at it. When she came into the room, people quietened down and simply looked to her to lead the group. Another one wasn't so good. He used to do a bit of shouting and wrote a lot of the stuff himself. He wasn't such a good leader.' Whatever your outside interests you should be able to adapt your answer to them.

BEING A TEAM PLAYER

A question often asked in this area – 'What sports are you interested in?' – is not idle banter to see what you do on Saturdays. They're looking for evidence of your involvement with groups. It helps them to know if it's likely that you can get along with people and pull together with a team. 'I really like team sports, particularly cricket. I played at school, and then at university I was the vice-captain of the seconds. My playing ability is a bit below my interest in the game, so I watch it a fair amount.'

Other sports that impress interviewers are stamina sports – swimming, running and cycling, for example. If you want to display your ability to analyse situations, pick bridge or chess. An associated question is, 'What did you learn from your holiday jobs?' Again, prepare to talk about leadership and teamwork.

You may want to put some of the material discussed here into IDEA 5, *Talk me briefly through your history.*

Try another idea...

'You live in a different world to me, Mr Overton, a sweeter and healthier one. My ramifications stretch out into many sections of society, but never, I am happy to say, into amateur sport, which is the best and soundest thing in England.'
ARTHUR CONAN DOYLE

Defining idea...

161

How did it go?

Q   **This topic came up and I answered truthfully that I love going fishing in different places. They responded with something like, 'Do you prefer working on your own or with others?' I knew that the job involved working in a team, so I said that I preferred working as part of a team pulling together. I could see that they thought these replies were inconsistent. What should I have done?**

A   *Probably added to your reply that you're also quite capable of working on your own and don't require much supervision; then the rest of your answer about pulling together works quite well. Most people at work spend too little time reflecting on what's going on and thus learning from experience. If you do enjoy lone sports like fishing, you can make the comment that it gives you lots of thinking time.*

Q   **I took your point and went back to playing tennis by rejoining my club. Do you think I should go on to the committee? No one wants to do it; so it would be easy enough. Would that help?**

A   *Probably. It depends on the rest of your CV. In any case you don't have to tell them that you can just walk on to the committee. In fact in this situation there's probably an opportunity. If no one wants to be on the committee you should be able to make a difference that you'll be able to talk about.*

38

Can we ask you to do a role-play and some group exercises?

The use of assessment centres to evaluate potential employees is widespread. Don't think you can't prepare for them.

As with any interview, have in mind the precise impression you want to leave behind. The clearer you have this impression in your mind, the better will be the filter through which you pass the decisions you have to make during the exercises.

Be a contributing member of the group but ration your contributions to times when they move the group forward. Be prepared to compromise and try not to go out on a limb unless you're absolutely sure you're right.

Here's an idea for you...

Think about the impression you want to leave behind when the interviews are over. Write this down so that you have it really well expressed. A good example is, 'I don't make rash decisions.' This will tend to lower the risks that you take at the centre. Now practise it. You can do this in normal meetings in your current job or you can ask other people to role-play with you. Then ask for feedback on the impression you made to see how accurately it mirrors your plan.

OK, TURN OVER YOUR PAPERS

Find out as much as you can about what the assessment centre will involve. Typically, you and the others will be given a group exercise where a team has to discuss a situation and come up with decisions about what to do next. The exercises will generally be relevant to the sort of job you're going for. If you're going for a sales job it will almost certainly involve a customer situation. If you're to become a team leader for the first time it's likely to involve handling a difficult team member. In all cases, look for an opportunity to suggest to the team how it might structure the discussion.

There are some basic communication rules for group discussion:

- It's easy to think that your contribution to a group discussion occurs when you're speaking. In fact in these group discussions it's often the person who says least who looks best. Listen to what people are saying, rather than spending your whole time preparing your next brilliant epigram.

- Don't interrupt people to get your point in. It's bad practice and rude, but you'll be amazed how much it happens.

- Look for occasions where you can support something that someone has just said: 'That was a really helpful contribution, Penny; thank you.'

IDEA 51, *How good are your time-management and presentation skills?* looks at other assessment centre exercises.

Try another idea...

- When someone has said something that you think has merit but needs more explanation, don't jump in and take it in your own direction. It's much better teamwork to ask them a clarifying question.

- When you know something about the group, you should be able to find an opportunity where, because of their background and experience, some people should be in a better position than others to make a contribution. It's very good team technique to invite such individuals to comment. This demonstrates skills in group discussion leadership: 'You know about the production side, Ellen. What do you think?'

WAIT TILL YOU CAN SEE THE WHITES OF THEIR EYES

Try not to jump into the discussion too early. It can be very effective to sit and listen hard to what's being said, asking questions and bringing people in appropriately.

Then form your view. Towards the end you can then give a comprehensive summary of the points that have been made and give your view or support someone else's view. With luck you may be instrumental in helping the group to come to an agreed decision.

'The reason we have two ears and only one mouth is that we may listen the more and talk the less.'
ZENO OF CITIUM

Defining idea...

THEY'RE ROLE-PLAYING; YOU'RE BEING YOURSELF

Try to look at role-play exercises in this way. If you're the salesperson and that's your job, then you're not role-playing; you're carrying out your function. Use the preparation time they give you. We know it's obvious, but do read the scenario meticulously. Generally, there's not much padding in the briefing; all the sentences and phrases are significant. So try not to miss anything. Try to connect the briefing to a real situation you've been in. It may not be that similar, but anything a bit like it can be helpful in making it feel real.

You're not on your own. If there's time, speak to other people at the centre to see what they make of the briefing. Ask the interviewers if you feel there is a piece of information that in real life you would have. They may decline to tell you, but it's worth trying. Take some deep breaths before you start. Go as slowly as you can. The temptation is to say too much too fast. Use open questions and try to relax. That's all there is to it.

At the end of an assessment centre session, the organisers have a lot of valuable data about you. Ask them for feedback. In most cases they'll give you it if you ask, but possibly not if you don't.

Q   I have a colleague who's been to an assessment centre. Would it
help me if I got her to talk about it and tell me what went on? Is it
a good idea when you're at the centre to phone people in the
outside world?

How did it go?

A   *It will probably help to discuss your colleague's experience. Get her to talk
about the feedback sessions as well as about what she had to do. Yes, it's
a great idea to get help from outside – that's what you'd do in real life.*

Q   If I don't take much part in the early part of the discussion, won't
that make the others look more like leaders than I will?

A   *No. Look at how good leaders handle group discussions and planning
meetings. They generally start by asking the group lots of questions.
Perhaps you shouldn't stay entirely quiet, but during the early stages try to
limit yourself to asking questions and bringing others in.*

39

It says in your CV that you took control of your last project when the project manager went sick. How did that go?

You must make your CV entirely consistent with what the interviewers will discover in interview. If you try to bluff them, they'll almost certainly trip you up and you'll have done yourself no favours.

This is a simple deal breaker. If they catch you out in a gross exaggeration or a lie, then you've probably blown it.

It's time to talk about bullshit. Take the example in the title of this Idea. If you've genuinely taken over for a significant length of time, then the statement is fair enough and you'll be able to substantiate it during the interview. If, however, the project manager had a couple of days off twice during the project, and you stood in for them at a couple of meetings, then your CV is misleading. The most you can claim is, 'I deputised from time to time for the project manager.' The Americans

Here's an idea for you...

Go over your CV with a fine-tooth comb. Challenge yourself to substantiate every claim you've made. If you feel that funnel questioning will catch you out, change the wording. You won't necessarily weaken your case and you remove the risk of looking as though you were trying to pull the wool over their eyes.

speak of a 'water cooler hero' when a junior member of a project tries to exaggerate their role by relying on the conversations the senior people had round the water cooler to bluff their way through.

THE FUNNEL TECHNIQUE

The way experienced interviewers expose such talk is to use the funnel technique. They stay very friendly as they ask one follow-up question after another until your cover is blown. It's extraordinary how often people fall at the first fence:

'I see it says on your CV that you measured the return on investment of sales campaigns before you submitted the proposal to the customer. How did that work?' 'Well, I had to work out the rate of return, taking into account the value of the sale and the costs involved in production, delivery and installation. It had to be at least 15% for me to be able to go ahead.'

'Was that just direct costs or overheads as well?'

'I'm not sure what you mean by that.'

'OK, let's talk about the rate of return. Did you do a cash flow and discount it, or how did you calculate it?'

'Well, actually it was the accountants who worked it out.'

'I see. What does a rate of return of 15% actually mean in your company?'

'Um, it was something to do with profitability.'

'Yes, of course. I understand. Next please.'

Defining idea...

'O what a tangled web we weave When first we practise to deceive.'
SIR WALTER SCOTT

The key is to be able to substantiate every statement you make on your CV and in answer to questions. They're never going to take big claims at face value; they're always going to squeeze you down the funnel as they go from wide open questions to become more and more specific.

IDEA 9, *Could you send me your CV please?* gives the detail of how to write a CV.

Try another idea...

MAKE SURE THAT WHAT THEY'VE SEEN IS WHAT THEY GET

Your CV covers not only what you've done in your life but also how you behave and what you're like. Your behaviour at the interview has to reflect that pen portrait. So, don't give yourself an impossible task by describing a person you cannot be. If you describe yourself as energetic and enthusiastic, that's how you must act. If you talk about your careful analysis of situations before you make decisions then you should be very thoughtful in answering their questions. If you think that they're looking for an outgoing personality for the job, then by all means write down that you have that quality – as long as you can quickly overcome any nervousness at the beginning and hit a good conversational stride.

When you're checking your CV, make sure that nothing that you've written could catch you out. Look out for adjectives; they're the words that trigger further questions. 'What exactly were the *tangible* benefits?' If you've described yourself as professional you've got to look and act the part. If you've written 'experienced coach and mentor', be prepared to discuss not only what you did but also the benefits to the person and the organisation of the coaching that you did.

'You told a lie, an odious damnèd lie: Upon my soul, a lie, a wicked lie!'
WILLIAM SHAKESPEARE

Defining idea...

How did it go?

Q **I'm leaving a company that is going through some very high-profile problems with financial and quality issues. The division I'm in has actually not done too badly. In fact, my part of the organisation made a good profit until it took on some of the costs of other divisions to make the whole look a bit better. Can I explain that, or will I just look as though I'm being shifty, when everyone knows about the parent company's problems?**

A *You should be OK telling the truth. Have as much information to substantiate what you're saying as you think does not breach confidentiality. People do realise that not every part of a company's awful when that company has problems.*

Q **I'm only twenty and when I went through my CV with your advice in mind I had to tone a lot down and cut a bit out. It looks very thin now. Don't you think I should risk some slight exaggeration? Won't it look as though I haven't done much, which could be worse?**

A *Leave it as the truth. It's much more risky to try to bluff. To be honest, no one has done much at your age anyway.*

172

40

How will you know when you've found the right job?

This is a useful question for both sides. Preparing for it gives you a huge insight into what you're really looking for. The interviewers may see a deal breaker in your criteria; or they may give them clues how to present the job to its best advantage.

The work you do in this area will pay off, not only in answering this question, but also in weighing the merits of any offer that may come along later.

You need a comprehensive set of criteria for your decision as to which job you want to take. You can really impress an interviewer when you answer this question if you demonstrate that you've used a logical system to come up with the criteria. You should also show that you've talked to everyone useful in deciding on the importance of each criterion.

Here's an idea for you... **There's a simple but very useful spreadsheet you can use in this area. Put potential employers across the top of your table. Now give each criterion a weighting, again between 1 and 10, where '10' is a very important criterion and '1' a 'nice to have'. Mark each employer as usual on the scale, but add another column for each employer and use it to multiply the score by the weighting. This enables you not only to check each job but also to compare it with others in a logical manner.**

WHAT ARE YOU GOING TO MEASURE?

First of all impress them with your organisation and preparation: 'I've taken four headings as my criteria: the type of organisation I want to work for, logistics such as remuneration, the impact of my job on my family and last but certainly not least the job satisfaction I think the role offers me.'

'OK, what type of organisation are you looking for?' Because you've come this far, it's likely that the one you're talking to has a lot of the attributes you've identified. Keep to the criteria for the moment and fill in the details when they ask the supplementary questions that are bound to arise. So, don't offer a heading if you can't substantiate it. Here's an outline of a possible response: 'I have to easily identify with the objectives of the organisation and the sector they operate in. I believe very much in "cultural fit". I've found that there are some organisations that I can easily operate with and others that are more difficult. I also want to go where there is success. I also need to feel that I can make the sort of contribution to that success that will stand out in the crowd.'

'So how do we measure up against those criteria?' You might answer, 'Very well. I like your long-term strategy of collaborative projects with other European companies and the fact that you're a leading light in the aerospace sector. From what I've gathered you operate a pretty free and easy, open and consultative culture. That suits my enjoyment of finding innovative solutions to problems. So, if I've read you right I think we could get on well and that I could really help the company to meet its financial and other goals.'

IDEA 14, Why do you want to work for this company? adds advice about the research you need to do in order to answer this question.

Try another idea...

Now move on to the other three. Keep the logistics bit short at this time. Unless they want to go into detail, it's better to impress them with the other bits of your research:

'As for logistics, I do want to use this change of job to improve my remuneration. I want to do my share of the travelling your people have to do; but I want to be home most weekends, and I'd like to be based in an office within, say, a half-hour's journey from home. In terms of job satisfaction, I want a stretching challenge and to work in a team that's enthusiastic about getting the job done. I want to use my project management skills as well as my engineering training and experience.'

HOW WILL YOU MEASURE THEM?

Now compile your list in a table under the four categories. Measure the importance of each on a scale of 1–10. Only use 10 for real deal breakers. You should have about four criteria in each area marked as particularly important. However, try not to put everything down as high priority. Most jobs will require some sort of compromise on some criteria.

'When you can measure what you are speaking about, and express it in numbers, you know something about it; but when you cannot measure it, when you cannot express it in numbers, your knowledge is of a meagre and unsatisfactory kind.'
LORD KELVIN

Defining idea...

How did it go?

Q   **OK, I've done all that and it was quite useful. The trouble is that I used the weightings as you suggest and one organisation comes up with a significant lead over the other; but instinctively the lower one feels right for me. It comes out OK in the exercise, just not as good as the other one. Should I let logic prevail or go with my gut?**

A   *Go with your gut. The exercise has helped you think the thing through, but in the end if you go with the logic and then don't particularly like it you'll regret not taking the other decision.*

Q   **I used your words about feeling that I could make a good financial contribution to the organisation and they came back with 'How?' I couldn't think of anything financial as I explained how well I could do the job. What is the answer to the 'How?' question?**

A   *Either use your experience on a previous job, or explain that you have always looked for tangible benefits in a cost/benefit analysis as part of your planning process. Remember that you're leading with your chin if you say something that you can't substantiate.*

41

Give me an example in your career where you felt like giving up and did

They're looking for a balance as usual. They want people with determination and tenacity; but they don't want you to keep banging your head against a brick wall.

How you explained to your boss what you thought needed to happen is as important as making the decision to halt a project.

Talk about your position when you realised that some objectives that you'd accepted became unachievable. Don't blame anyone. Rather, look at the circumstances that changed or a judgement that proved wrong, with the result that continuing the project was not good for the company, your team or you.

PROTECT THE COMPANY FROM SENDING GOOD MONEY AFTER BAD

Explain the project, what went wrong and how you recovered the situation as far as was possible: 'I was asked by my company to take the technological product I was

Here's an idea for you...

If you don't have an example in this area, it may not be too late to manufacture one. Have a really comprehensive look at the interfaces you have with other parts of the organisation. Is there any place where, simply to protect your empire or status, you're continuing a process that probably should be removed or changed? Now see if it would be a good idea to propose, in a short report, that the change should be made. Doing so before the organisation realises that it needs to change is good for your current career and a great story for an interview.

selling in Europe and try to develop a new market in the US. We knew it was a huge opportunity and we knew that the product at the time was pretty competitive. They gave me some good people and a budget that reflected the size of the opportunity. I knew it was risky, in that breaking into America is never easy; but the upside looked worth the attempt. With hindsight we needed much more local knowledge and probably one or two Americans at a higher level in the new subsidiary that we hired. We encountered competition in New York State on a scale greater than in the whole of Europe. We encountered scepticism about "the Brits selling technology in the States". It took a long time to get the first order and by then, nearly a year into the project, I knew we were never going to succeed in the way we were set up. I wrote a report saying that if we wanted to get into the States we needed to form a partnership with a local company or find some other way of tackling the new market. My boss didn't want to give up. She knew that the Chief Executive was keen on the project and she offered me further funds and resources to give it another year. I flew home and had a long meeting with her, detailing the situation. In the end she agreed. We pulled the team back – they were highly relieved – and went back to the drawing board.'

This has the elements you want. You take responsibility, you call a halt at the right time and you inform your boss of your recommendation. You also suggest how to tackle the task in a different way that might be successful. Perhaps most importantly, you don't just keep going to please your boss and the Chief Executive. You're plainly putting the company first.

The other side of this balance is discussed in IDEA 24, *Give me an example in your career where you felt like giving up but managed to keep going.*

Try another idea...

YOUR PROJECT OR MINE

Companies sometimes, by accident or design, run a number of parallel projects, knowing that they will in the end choose one as the long-term strategy. It happens in product development and the location of manufacturing plants, for example. In such situations it's easy for the project managers of 'competing' projects to get so entrenched that they battle to defend their operation way beyond where the interests of the company lie.

You should be able to find a small or big example from your career as an illustration of this. Perhaps you were just scrapping for the same office facilities with another group; or trying to maintain the mix of accounts on your sales patch. Look at where you decided that it was in the company's interests for you to back down and you've got a good story for this question.

'Because many professionals are almost always successful at what they do, they rarely experience failure. And because they have rarely failed, they have never learnt how to learn from failure.'
CHRIS ARGYRIS, Harvard Business School professor

Defining idea...

179

How did it go?

Q **I had a story quite like your example to tell. I was asked a similar question in an interview and told the story much as you suggested. One of the managers then came at me quite aggressively, saying that I had plainly accepted an objective that turned out to be unachievable. To some extent he was right, of course. So can you ever say that a professional manager should ever have something go badly wrong? Surely they should have seen it coming.**

A *In our dreams, yes. Perhaps your response didn't dwell enough on the risk to the success of the project which you knew you were taking. That might have softened their attack. But in any case, a big return generally carries a big risk; and most highly successful people have sometime taken a big risk – that has or hasn't come off.*

Q **I did give up on a project, but after the dust had settled it became obvious that I had gone on with it too long. The trouble is that just when I was thinking that I should recommend we should call it a day, something would happen that gave us all hope again. Should I explain this or does it sound bad?**

A *It's certainly something that happens all the time. George Brown described it as being like sitting in a bath with the water going up by half a degree at a time. Eventually you end up scalded. You can probably use the example and then show what you learnt from it.*

42

Is it all right if we take up your references now?

The days when employers didn't bother to check on references are long over. There are some referees whom you can use and some whom you must.

References are slightly dangerous things. They're unlikely to get you the job, but they could lose you it. So think them through carefully.

There is, of course, only one answer to this question. Take it as a buying sign. The interviewers are not going to take up references of people they've already decided not to take. So smile confidently. 'Yes, that's fine. They're briefed that you might be getting in touch with them.'

USE THE QUESTION AS A LEVER

There are some circumstances when you can demur from giving referees' names out – where you're applying for a job without your current employer knowing about it, for example; or where you don't want a referee to know to whom you're applying unless it's extremely likely that you'll join them.

Here's an idea for you... If you haven't already done so, make a list of potential referees and get in touch with them. Ask them to write letters of recommendation. You'll probably find that some of them, if not all, will agree to discuss what you want them to put in the document before they write it. This is very useful, since you can use them to back up the main points you're going to make when you're answering the question, 'Why should we offer you this job?'

In both these cases you can use the request as an opportunity to test the water and push them along a bit: 'Yes, of course I'm happy for you to take up references; but I don't want to alert my two main referees that we're talking unless we've made good progress and there's a good chance that we might be going ahead together. I wonder if this is the right time now, or if you think we should wait for a bit?'

With regard to your current employer you can go even further: 'I would prefer to give my current employer as a referee only when you have made me an offer that I have accepted. We should also have agreed a start date so that I can resign in a professional way and leave a good taste behind me when I leave.'

WHO DO YOU USE?

There's one referee you must use and that's your previous or current boss. If you don't, the sceptical interviewer will fear the worst. So even if they've moved on, track them down and get them to agree to act. In fact, whenever you move jobs, or start to apply for another one, speak to your boss about a reference. Ask them what they would say. Everybody knows how important it is; so most reasonable people will not only tell you what they will say but might even write it down there and then and show you it.

It's a good idea to gather a few of these recommendations as your career progresses so that you can pull out a bunch of good opinions whenever someone asks for one.

The best way to be confident about any referee is to get an advance copy of what they would say in a general recommendation and to get them to copy you the one they actually send in response to the organisation's request. Frequently, this is on a pre-prepared form.

IDEA 22, *What opinion have you formed of the people you've met so far?* warns you about speaking about other people.

Try another idea…

A slightly quirky, and often excellent, referee is someone who has worked for you rather than the other way around. They'll say something about what it's like to work for you and what they liked about it.

If you're looking for your first job, it's still best to have someone for whom you've done some work. The shop manager where you had your Saturday job or the warehouse you worked at during college vacations will do pretty well. If there really isn't anyone whom you've worked for (not even as a babysitter?) you might have to fall back on personal referees. Human resources departments are not terribly impressed with personal references, since you can choose the one you want as opposed to having to choose one from your working past.

When you're talking to a potential referee, remember the three areas you want them to comment on:

- leadership: your drive, energy and self-insight
- job function: your technical capabilities in doing the job
- future potential: your relationships with others and your ambition for the future.

'You will find it a very good practice always to verify your references, sir!'
MARTIN JOSEPH ROUTH, British classicist

Defining idea…

183

How did it go?

Q **I don't quite understand this. I'm in a very delicate situation. I'm applying to the main competitor of the company I work for just now. I don't quite know what my employer would do if I, or the company I'm applying to, let them in on the secret. So I thought it was good advice to say that I wouldn't give them the reference until we had agreed when I would start. Doesn't that mean that my current employer's reference is irrelevant?**

A *It could be. But more likely is that your potential new employer will make the offer dependent on getting satisfactory references.*

Q **I want to use a recommendation that I got from a holiday job employer a year ago. Subsequently he discovered that some of the students who worked for him had been taking time off and doing much less than he had thought. He's somewhat tarring us all with the same brush although I've assured him that I wasn't among the slackers. Is it dangerous to use the old recommendation?**

A *I'm afraid so. If the interviewer gets in touch with the man having seen his recommendation and gets a different story from him at that time, it could be serious enough for them to stop considering you. Rack your brains and think of someone else.*

43

What other roles are you considering, and how does this one stack up?

They want to know how well they're doing in attracting you. It's one of a number of questions concerning your job mobility.

You can't just say that such questions are none of their business; but you do have to politely but firmly sidestep one or two of them.

They're looking for someone who sees the opportunity as a good role into which they could settle down, make a good contribution and stay long enough to make a difference. Always end answers to questions like these with a positive statement about your intentions in those three areas. They're also checking that you're taking this career change seriously, that you've thought out how to go about it and that you have a good plan of action.

Here's an idea for you...

The most difficult area in any CV is a long gap when you were out of work. Interviewers may ask about this quite assertively. The only sure way of delivering a smooth, convincing answer is to try it out in role-play. Get someone to probe hard and ask difficult supplementary questions as you justify the gap. Always end positively about the job you're discussing. 'I've wanted to make sure that my next move is absolutely the right one for my career and personal development, so I'm not rushing into anything; but I think I've found what I'm looking for in this job.'

THEY'RE COMPETING TOO

Tell them exactly what you're doing unless there is a huge reason not to do so. This reassures them that you're serious: 'I am looking at a few other things. The main thing I've discovered is that the opportunities I can go for are all very different jobs with their own unique attributes. It's like trying to compare apples and pears. I'm certainly very interested in the job we're discussing here.' They may say, 'Why?' so be prepared to state what you regard as the job's best unique attribute.

One question on job mobility is, 'I see you've changed jobs pretty frequently, including one where you only stayed for six months. Why haven't you settled down?' It's probably OK to have job-hopped a bit in your youth – even interviewers were young once – so the key here is to explain why you're now thinking of settling down. Try to keep your reasons for changing jobs positive rather than negative.

'I was happy in my first job, but got the opportunity to do a similar role in a company where the journey to work was much shorter. That second job went well. Then I got what seemed like a big opportunity in a start-up company. With the benefit of hindsight, that was a mistake: the company didn't get off the ground properly and I left after six months. I've been with my present company for a while now; so I don't think I've job-hopped too much. Besides, I've got good and varied experience out of each job I've done. But you're right. I do think it's time that I settled down into a company that can offer me good personal development and a long-term career. That's why I'm here.'

There another idea on negotiating in IDEA 52, *Surely the gap between what you want and what we're offering isn't significant enough to stop you taking the job?*

Try another idea...

They might also probe to see if your expectation of changing jobs in their organisation is unrealistic: 'When do you expect your first promotion to come along?' Be careful with this one. Balance your ambition to get ahead with their need to get a satisfactory job done in the role they're offering you: 'I know it's always hard to tell with these things; so I suppose the answer is, "When the time is right." I know I have to settle into this job first. I mean, you aren't going to offer me a promotion until I've come up with a performance that merits a step up.'

MAKE THEM SELL AGAIN

If you are in the happy position of having two jobs that you find equally satisfactory, you can use this question to solicit the best offer that you can: 'I'm looking at another job that has good potential like the one we're talking about. They see the role as a bit more senior than you do here; so it's a slightly higher status and the remuneration is a bit higher too. However, I really like the career development opportunities in what we're discussing.' Adding the last sentence makes sure that it doesn't look as though you're putting a gun to their heads.

'There are no short cuts to the top. There is one thing worse than not getting to where you want to go and that is not being equipped once you get there.'
SIR CHRISTOPHER HOGG, British executive

Defining idea...

How did it go?

Q   **I've been out of work for nearly a year; I've applied for a lot of jobs and I've had no offers whatsoever. How do I handle that situation in an interview?**

A   *Explain that you've been looking hard for the right opportunity. You were tempted by some possibilities but decided to hold out for a job that met all your criteria. End up by suggesting that with this one you hope you've found it.*

Q   **I talked about another higher offer I have with another company. They said that what was on the table was the best they could do at present. I asked them if they would review the situation once they'd seen my work. I've now been here six months, they're telling me I'm doing a great job but there's no sign of a review. The trouble is that my boss has changed, so the person I spoke to in the interview isn't there any more. How could I have avoided this?**

A   *The only thing you could have done was to make them be more specific about when they would do the review when you were in the interview. You could then ask them to write it into the job offer. People will often do that if they feel they're talking to the right person for the job.*

44

Would you say you're a glass-half-empty person or a glass-half-full?

For most interviewers a positive mental attitude is almost an obsession. Find a way of displaying yours, and talk about the difference it can make.

It's true that the attitude with which we approach events does have an impact on how things turn out.

If we wish to perform at our best and to help others do the same we need to start from the attitude that everyone is equipped with the ability to succeed. Now, how do you get that into the answer to an interview question?

WE CAN MAKE IT HAPPEN

What's behind this question is a rather negative probe. The supplementary questions are likely to be in the area of how you handle setbacks and how you behave when things are not going as well as they might. So start with a huge smile

Here's an idea for you... **Take a task that you have to perform and that you are not looking forward to. Firstly, remember that it is your choice whether or not to do the task. Now imagine having completed the task and that you enjoyed doing it. Next, set aside the time to do the task – the sooner the better. Choose to be positive about the job rather than downbeat. If you start off feeling negative it will make the task much more of a chore you can't enjoy. Try it; it works.**

and an assurance that you are naturally a very positive person. Then use an example of someone you have known who passes that attitude on to others. Try to give examples of what they did, to show that the attitude comes out in real activities as opposed to anything that's airy-fairy.

'At heart I'm definitely an optimist. I've worked with both types of people. I've worked with a team leader who was a terrible pessimist and moaner. He was always criticising the company and the people in it. I had to keep reminding myself that nothing was as bad as he was making out; but some people in the team got infected with the glass-half-empty bug, and didn't enjoy their work. I know our performance suffered as a result. I've also worked with a woman who was the opposite. She refused to use the word "problem", and put messages on the board saying, for example, that "I can't" or "we can't" were both banned phrases. We all expected to succeed in her environment and we did.'

This is an area where an analogy with sport can be useful: 'It's interesting when you consider sport. There's an obvious phenomenon that champion sides win even when they're not playing very well. I think it's something to do with the fact that they're simply expecting to win. The "positive mental attitude" that sports coaches talk about does have an effect.'

AND WHEN THE GOING GETS TOUGH?

A person who expects everything to go right at work is not an incurable optimist so much as a fool. They'll probe for your response to adversity. 'How do you handle rejection?' This is particularly asked of customer-facing people in a competitive industry. If they can't handle losing a few then they should be in another profession: 'I think that being rejected from time to time is part of the process of being a salesperson. After all, if every customer said 'yes' the company wouldn't need a sales force in the first place. I try to take responsibility for a loss without taking it as a personal rejection. That way I can move on knowing that I'm one campaign closer to my next sale.'

Another way to probe for negativity is, 'Why do you want to leave your job?' It's quite possible to answer this one positively, even though you are leaving because of the lack of something. Just show how there is nothing anyone can do about your reason for leaving: 'It's a small business. I've learnt what I can from it and there is no advancement possible.' Or: 'The job was interesting when I started, and I've enjoyed doing it and being successful; but I think the time has come to tackle something more challenging.'

Look at this question in terms of a team with IDEA 49, *The division you'd be managing has its head right down at the moment: how will you set about re-motivating them?*

Try another idea…

'You've got to ac-cent-tchu-ate the positive
Elim-my-nate the negative
Latch on to the affirmative
Don't mess with Mr In-between.'
JOHNNY MERCER, US songwriter

Defining idea…

How did it go?

Q **I tried the positive mental attitude bit and it proved very intriguing. I had to take a trip to a customer that involved catching busy trains, changing twice, not being able to park at the station and so on. And at the end of the journey I knew I would be facing a far from satisfied customer. So I tried this thing out. I imagined everything about the journey going well, and the discussion with the customer proceeding in a way that produced a very positive outcome. Guess what? It went like a dream! Isn't that amazing?**

A *Yes, it's interesting isn't it? It's also why we put some tasks off and then find when we do tackle them that there wasn't much difficult about them at all. Anyway you've got a good story to tell the interviewer if a question like this comes up. Just one thing: don't make it sound metaphysical or spiritual. That goes down well with some people, but others hate it.*

Q **I'm a salesman and I got the rejection question. I answered much as you suggested and a sales manager suggested that if I didn't feel bad, either I wasn't expecting success or I didn't feel that it was because of what I'd done that I didn't get the business. How should I have handled that?**

A *Perhaps you need a little introduction to your positive attitude, such as, 'Well, I wouldn't be human if it didn't hurt when someone chooses not to buy; but I've learnt not to let it get me down for more than a moment.'*

45

What are your strengths and weaknesses?

This is a very general question that you should expect. It deserves a well-prepared answer. You need to demonstrate not only a high level of self-insight but also corroborating evidence from other people.

This is an example of a double question, often used by HR people: 'What's positive about...and what's negative about...?'

For each planned assertion of a strength or weakness, think of a supplementary question they might ask. Often the real test is these supplementary questions, so you have to prepare for them.

I'M GOOD; I'M VERY, VERY GOOD

Start with a general statement of what you are and what you do. Then show what strengths you had to have to achieve the results you have: 'I'm an energetic IT professional with experience in running complex projects. I have a proven record of delivering the benefits of technology to a business. I have run teams as big as thirty and have had to involve many other people in the organisation in order to

Here's an idea for you...

Good interviewers are adept at getting to your strengths and weaknesses – through what they've read about you and through the interview process. It's vital, therefore, that you do have good insights into the real you. Take all of your appraisals – you have kept them, haven't you? – and list the strengths and weaknesses that the appraisers have picked out. There will be a pattern that you should take very seriously. When you've finished your preparation for this question, go over your answer with somebody senior to you who knows you well. You may as well have their insights too.

implement computer projects. During that time I developed my strengths in a number of areas. First, I'm very commercially minded. I never forget that IT is there to serve the financial performance of the organisation. (I've had to convert some people who start from the opposite position – that the organisation is there to benefit the smooth running of the IT department.) After I delivered my last project the managing director went on record as saying that the project had saved the company millions of dollars in currency transactions.

'I have strong project management and control skills; but I recognise that all the project management tools in the world don't get the work done. People do that. I enjoy leading teams and I have skills in involving and motivating the people in them. My last boss will testify to that and two of my referees are people who've been in teams I've managed. Most of the projects I've done have meant that a lot of people have had to change how they work. There's often heavy resistance to change and my tenacity when things are difficult has been fully tested. A departmental manager for whom I implemented a new system believes that I had at one point more people trying to hinder my delivering the system than I had helping me. Having said that, another strength I have is flexibility. If I have to change course I can do so rapidly in order to meet a new demand.' Notice the pattern: the result, the strengths necessary to achieve that result and finally the evidence from a third party.

Another way of putting the question is, 'What would you say are your outstanding qualities?' You can probably structure your answer in a similar way. If you choose to talk more personally try not to give them a simple list. It's much stronger to pick out one or two qualities and tell a story illustrating the benefits of those particular qualities.

IDEA 34, *In your current role what has been your major disappointment?* looks at the good use of words to answer questions about weaknesses.

Try another idea...

BUT IF I HAVE A WEAKNESS...

Choose weaknesses that are based on truth. Remember they're looking for self-insight, but choose weaknesses that in fact will probably benefit the organisation rather than hinder it: 'I've discussed with my manager a couple of areas that I need to think about and work on improving. If I have a team member who's struggling with something, I tend if I'm not careful to jump in and do the job for them rather than leave them to develop their skills. I do this sometimes when time is short. I need to put in place good training and development plans to make sure I don't do this. Although I appreciate the importance of my work/life balance to both the quality of my life and my accomplishments at work, I do sometimes overbalance towards work. Both I and my family are working on this.'

Finish off by using the term 'weakness' in its alternative meaning to end with a bit of humour. 'I also have a weakness for the Scottish rugby team. It's sad, I know, but I'm afraid incurable.'

'O! it is excellent to have a giant's strength, but it is tyrannous to use it like a giant.'
WILLIAM SHAKESPEARE

Defining idea...

How did it go?

Q **I've looked through my old appraisals and found an inconsistency. One person talks about my strength in presentation skills, particularly my ability to think on my feet, change course a bit if necessary and still achieve the objective of the presentation. Someone else talking in the same area said that I relied on my presentation skills to get me out of potential problems I could possibly have avoided by doing more preparation. So, what do I do?**

A *Celebrate! You've found a double answer to the double question. Tell them about the skills as a strength, and show them that you're very careful not to take it for granted that these will get you through. You've learnt that you still have to do all the preparation work to make sure.*

Q **Look, I don't suffer fools gladly. You talk as though that should be called a weakness. I intend to talk about it as a strength. Why shouldn't I?**

A *We wish you a happy life, in which you neither meet, nor work with, nor work for any fools. The rest of us try to overcome the weakness of being impatient with less competent people by working to develop their capabilities.*

46

Would it be OK for you to go and see our occupational psychologist?

A growing number of companies are using the services of psychologists to check a person's fit into their organisation. Such psychologists mainly test and interview people applying for senior jobs.

You've got to see this for the huge opportunity it is. Someone's spending money in a way that will tell you a lot about yourself.

There is only one answer to this question and that's 'yes'. Not only do you have to get over this hurdle to join the organisation, but you'll get very interesting feedback about yourself from attending such sessions. They're less nerve-racking if you know a bit about these people and what they do.

WHO ARE THESE PEOPLE?

First of all they're well qualified. They have a first degree in general psychology and possibly a master's degree in occupational psychology. They then go through

Here's an idea for you...

When you've done your preparation for this interview, check it over with as many people as is practical and useful. In particular, go over it with your brothers and sisters. It's extraordinary how siblings remember their common childhood in different ways, and you'll get lots of useful self-insight from such a discussion. You'll also get reliable answers to questions about what you have inherited from your parents.

practical training under the supervision of a chartered occupational psychologist. So whatever results their tests and interviews come up with, it's hugely useful for you to get such an informed opinion of what you're like and what sort of teams and organisations you fit well with.

As well as providing evaluations of candidates, psychologists may be involved in every aspect of the employer's recruitment process. They can monitor and validate selection procedures and design shortlisting methods to identify candidates with the potential required for particular jobs. They identify training needs and develop and evaluate training programmes, particularly those involved in how to get the best out of others and out of ourselves.

THE BIOGRAPHICAL INTERVIEW

An occupational psychologist is expert in detecting from the life history of a person what their main personal attributes are. They're looking for quite soft data such as, 'Is this person creative?' or 'How resilient is this person? Let's be clear: if it's difficult enough to mislead an experienced HR interviewer by skating over facts or being dishonest, then how much more difficult will it be to pull the wool over the eyes of someone whose entire training and experience have been aimed at getting to the core persona of their clients? Be as open and honest as you can. Take a positive attitude into the interview. Remember other people pay a lot of money to go to a psychologist to gain more self-knowledge. So enjoy it and you'll get a lot out of it.

The way the psychologists operate it is to ask open questions about all aspects of your life, including your upbringing. They will ask, for example, 'In what ways would you say that you are similar to your mother and father?' So, preparation work for this interview is to think hard about your relationships, particularly those in the early, formative part of your life. They may also ask, 'What is your earliest memory?' There's nothing to do except rack your brains and tell them what it is.

Now think of extremes of happiness and sadness you've experienced. What caused these feelings? Think not only about when you were happy at work but also about when you were happy for a length of time in work and leisure. Think about stress. In what circumstances do you feel stress? Try, in short, to take as objective a view of yourself as you possibly can. Finally, think about questions such as, 'What sort of a person are you?' and, 'Who is the real you?'

It's best to ask beforehand how you will be debriefed on the results of the process. You're probably in a slightly stronger position to negotiate the amount of feedback you'll get than if you wait to ask until after the interview. The ideal, of course, would be to have your own interview with the occupational psychologist who met you so that you can use them in another of their guises – career planning and training and development planning.

IDEA 13, *Would you mind taking a simple test to see how you might fit in with your colleagues?* looks at assessment centres, which are often designed by occupational psychologists.

Try another idea...

'Any man who goes to a psychiatrist needs his head examining.'
SAM GOLDWYN, US film-maker

Defining idea...

Don't make an appointment to do anything in the least bit difficult after the interview. You will be absolutely drained; answering their questions is hard but very interesting work. Nota bene: psychologists are not psychiatrists; they're not involved in diagnosing or treating psychological disorders.

How did it go?

Q **It didn't go very well, as a matter of fact. I did the tests and had the interview and was told by the employer that my profile didn't really fit. Not only did it not fit with their organisation but it didn't really fit with the occupation I've been in for seven years. In the politest possible way they told me I'm in the wrong job. I think it's right for me, I've been reasonably successful, but are they right?**

A *It looks as though the feedback session you were given wasn't handled very well. Maybe you're reading too much into it; but it's bad luck and, we're sure, quite unsettling. Make sure you get the details and proper feedback from the psychologist who conducted the interview.*

Q **I had a long chat with my sister and she disagreed – quite amicably, I hasten to say – with some of my comparisons of me with my parents. I feel confused now. What shall I say in response to a question about me and my parents?**

A *Unless your sister has completely convinced you, perhaps you should give both opinions. Say what you think is the case and then balance this with the alternative from your sister.*

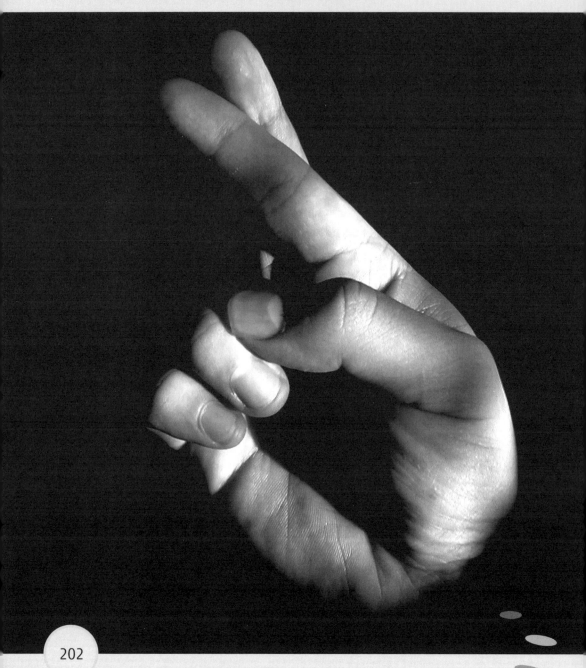

47

How do you go about making an important decision?

They're looking for method here, checking that you've thought about decision making per se and that you look at a situation from all angles before you decide what to do.

In answering this question, never forget that a decision is not really finalised until the actions that flow from it have well and truly started.

It's another balancing act. On the one hand you have to be seen as making a major decision in a structured, logical way. Your process must ensure you don't, for example, miss the best option available. On the other hand they don't want to see a love of bureaucracy that makes your decision making so process oriented that it stifles flair and intuition. And it has to have a shortcut version that allows you to come to a rough conclusion quickly.

EXPLAINING THE PROCESS

Fundamentally, an important decision is one that affects a lot of people and/or involves a lot of money. A decision is also important if getting it wrong could have a hugely detrimental impact on the company. Explain your process and demonstrate

Here's an idea for you... **If you explain a process to the interviewer they're bound to follow up with, 'Give me an example of a time when you've gone through that process.' It's a good idea, therefore, to take a key decision that you or your team made and write down an analysis of this process so that you've got a great example to talk about.**

that you can do it fast when necessary: 'I was fortunate in being taught a decision-making process on a training course. I've modified it a bit, mainly to make sure that it doesn't take too long to reach a final decision. I find it better to go through this process with a team, but it's quite possible to do it on my own. We first agree what we've got to make a decision about. Then we go through four steps:

'We identify the issues, the problems or opportunities, around the topic. We take care to understand as accurately as possible the impact each issue has on performance.

'From there we move to discussing the options. This is when flair and lateral thinking are at their most effective. That's why it's so useful to do it in a team: you never know who may come up with a new option.

'When we're sure we've identified all the options, we evaluate them. I get the team to agree what the selection criteria should be. There might be a criterion that the chosen solution must require very few extra people in the team to implement it. Then we systematically mark each of the options on a scale of 1–10 on each criterion. This gives us a good measure to compare options. We can also decide which criteria are the most important to us.

'This gives a good logical platform on which to make the decision. Through bitter experience I've found that decision making mustn't stop there. You then have to agree the action plan and decide who's responsible for each action. That way you make sure that your brilliant decision actually gets implemented.

'I've used that process often enough to be able to go through it quickly if I have to make a quick decision.' They may ask, 'Do you think it's important to document all this analytical work?' You reply, 'Crucial; otherwise you find that you haven't tied off all the loose ends and everyone involved has a different view of the decision and how it was made. Documentation makes it possible for other people to learn from the process you went through and is useful for evaluating the decision-making process after the dust has settled.'

There's more on risk in IDEA 25, Where have you made your organisation take a big risk?

Try another idea...

WHAT ABOUT RISK?

If you haven't mentioned the word 'risk' in your reply, it'll probably come up in a supplementary question: 'How do you take risk into account?' Describe a similar process for risk analysis: 'We identify everything that could go wrong in implementing the decision and estimate the probability of the risk occurring and the impact on performance if it does. This gives a quick and accurate picture of the most significant risks. The team can then agree actions to mitigate the key risks.'

'Wherever you see a successful business someone once made a courageous decision.'
PETER DRUCKER, management consultant

Defining idea...

'Ever notice that "What the hell" is always the right decision?'
MARILYN MONROE

Defining idea...

How did
it go?

Q **I tried this with a horrible result. I went through your process in retrospect on a decision that I and another woman took about three months ago. First we thought of some other options. Then we found that the decision we'd actually taken came third in the evaluation. The interview's tomorrow so I've got to fix it. How?**

A *Take each of the criteria and give it a weighting, making sure that the highest weighting goes to the criteria that your actual decision scored highest in. Now multiply the scores on the criteria by the weighting to give the weighted average. Keep adjusting the weightings until your decision soars above the rest. You'll need to have good arguments for how you chose the weightings in case they ask about that too.*

Q **When I was trying to get some more money out of the advertising director, I asked her if she agreed with how I was evaluating the decision and she said yes but that she wanted to add another criterion. This rather threw me, since the one she chose didn't really favour the decision I was promoting. I stuttered and stammered to try to fit the new criterion in. Isn't this going to happen quite often?**

A *Possibly, but if she had not come up with the new criterion then it would have emerged as an objection to your decision later on. Take a careful note of the new criterion and make sure you have understood exactly what the director is looking for. Then go back to your decision. You have till the end of the meeting to think out how to deal with the new issue. That's more time than you'd have had if the issue had come up as an objection.*

48

What reservations would you have if we offered you the role?

This question could offer room for negotiation. It's also a direct request for information. What you say could, of course, affect whether or not they actually make the offer.

Don't forget the rule that covers all interview answers — always start with a positive.

Tackle this in three ways: first, what you like about the job, second, a strategic reservation about taking the job and finally, something to encourage them to make their best offer or to alter the job's conditions to your advantage.

THERE'S SOMETHING THEY CAN'T PUT RIGHT

The psychology towards the end of an interview is interesting. Both sides can start to believe that there is an exact fit: they just want you to do the job, and you can't believe that this is so like the job you want. This is sometimes called the 'halo effect'. Don't succumb to it. Go back over the criteria you've set yourself and check that this job is right for you.

Here's an idea for you... **Before you go into the final interview or if they've asked you back to dot the i's and cross the t's of your joining letter, refine the detail of your criteria for taking the job. What's different between what you originally wanted and what they're offering? Is there anything else that would make the job even more perfect? The original criteria you used when deciding whom to apply to and whom to go and see may well be out of date. You need to have the new list firmly in your head to tackle this question to your full advantage.**

'I really like what I've understood about the job from my research, my observation of what goes on here and from the interview process. The challenge looks terrific and I'm certain I can handle it and do a good job. When I first started looking, however, I thought I would stay in the banking area at this stage in my career. It's what I've known for a while now. But I'm still very attracted to the job we're discussing.'

Now you can just ask for time to think about it. After all, an offer in the hand is useful even if just as a benchmark for other possibilities: 'What I've learnt about the civil service has certainly changed my mind in a number of ways and perhaps that reservation is more a misunderstanding than a deal breaker.' Now wait for their response. They may offer to let you have a further look around, or to fill any knowledge gap propose some training. It's useful to keep quiet at some moments and let them decide where to take the conversation.

There's another question in this area that you mustn't let throw you: 'What do you think will be the least interesting part of the job?' The safe route is to take something that no one in any job likes doing and make a joke of it. They may not be happy about anything else that you might mention, so play the percentage shot: 'Keeping the hard copy filing up to date is not my favourite time of the week; but I do know it's got to be done.'

If there lurks in the back of your mind a real reservation about your ability to do the job, or if you feel that in one area you've oversold your skills and knowledge, this is a good time to air the matter. The worst that can happen is that they don't offer you a job that you couldn't in any case handle, which is no bad thing. The best that can happen is that they become aware you're going to need help or training in that area.

IDEA 40, *How will you know when you've found the right job?* gives advice on how to draw up a table of your decision criteria and put weightings on them.

Try another idea...

AND SOMETHING THEY CAN

Unless you think it's insensitive, like if you think it might wreck the euphoria of the moment, pop in a negotiable point here: 'The only logistics thing that troubles me is travelling into West London everyday. I had been hoping to work at home at least one day of the week.' Use the moment when they're making a job offer to negotiate the best terms and conditions possible.

'I take the official oath today with no mental reservations, and with no purpose to construe the Constitution or laws by any hypercritical rules.'
ABRAHAM LINCOLN

Defining idea...

How did it go?

Q **I knew that my spreadsheet skills would be under pressure in the new job; so I told the interviewers I had a reservation in that area and expressed my keenness to get some training in the subject. Although the senior woman and the HR guy seemed OK with this, and indeed did talk about providing training, my potential boss looked quite put out. He definitely damped down the other people's enthusiasm and I thought all was lost. Eventually they all agreed that it wasn't a deal breaker; but it was a near thing, so are you sure about your advice in this particular area?**

A *You've got the job and no one can say that you misled them about your spreadsheet skills, least of all your boss. You should be able to motivate him to get you some training the moment you go on board. Incidentally, are you sure you hadn't purposely or perhaps by accident suggested earlier that you knew more about spreadsheets than you do? Have a look at what your CV hints at in this area.*

Q **If they ask me this question my only real reservation concerns the bloke that I'll have to work for. He doesn't look that smart to me. Should I find a form of words to say that to them?**

A *Possibly. You could have tried asking the question, 'What are you like to work for?' This will give you more evidence. Think about life with that person. Will you be happy working there? Then make a decision, because if you express doubts about your boss's competence right from the start you're asking for trouble. Best avoid the job if it's a big problem.*

49

The division you'd be managing has its head right down at the moment: how will you set about re-motivating them?

A fair and difficult question. Answer with a process to fix the immediate problems, and a plan for boosting motivation in the long term.

Remember that the members of the team at the coalface are the best people to ask for ideas to improve matters.

This is not an uncommon situation. The team needs a new leader perhaps because the old one didn't get them to perform to their best or achieve their objectives. The new leader faces more than the normal problems of taking on a new team – wariness about a stranger and so on.

Here's an idea for you… If you haven't facilitated a team planning session you should do so. It's extraordinary the insights such a meeting can produce. Keep it simple; start from a general statement of what the team is trying to achieve. Document the strengths, weaknesses, opportunities and threats the team faces in achieving results. This identifies the issues the team needs to address. Set objectives for improving matters and make a clear action plan. Don't believe the miseries who say that strategic planning is difficult. A manager needs to be able to show experience in this area when going for a new job or promotion.

THE FIRST FEW WEEKS

Start your answer with an assurance that you'll put a lot of effort into this crucial part of your role: 'I'd recognise the importance of spending a huge amount of time with the team, talking to them and getting to know them. I'd use that time to analyse thoroughly what the problems are as the team see them; why they're not feeling good about their work.'

You may then get the question, 'What do you think are the likely causes of poor team morale?' You might reply, 'In my experience it frequently starts from a communications problem. The team doesn't feel that management are keeping them informed. This often happens if a manager is trying not to worry a team with some problems the organisation has. This never works. They're not fools and they know something's going on; so they worry, even though they don't know the details. I'd make sure as quickly as I can that they hear the full story of the organisation's position and theirs in it.

'The other main cause of team demotivation is lack of involvement in the decision-making process. If their views are not taken into account when plans are made they're going to feel unhappy. I find that the best people to find a way round problems or improve a difficult situation are usually the people at the coalface. If you want to know how to sell more product and services ask the salespeople. If you need to reduce direct costs ask the people in production. I use a structured but simple team planning process that makes certain that everyone contributes to planning the way ahead.' Be prepared for a supplementary question on planning processes.

IDEA 30, *What really gets you up in the morning looking forward to work?* offers more on this area.

Try another idea...

AND THEN FOREVER

'How do you keep your team wanting to come to work in the morning?' One possible answer: 'I find that resolving issues quickly is best done by assigning teams of, say, two people to find solutions. This is stronger than an individual working on their own with occasional input from their leader. I also know how important to a team is a wide perspective of what's going on in the organisation. I make sure they know how important they and their work are to the whole organisation – that's a huge motivator. I believe that bonuses and rewards are part of motivating a team but by no means the whole of it. I understand the crucial importance of appreciating their efforts – they need regular praise and thanks. Sometimes it's good to set monthly goals so that the team can get together more frequently to celebrate their achievements. I also find that people need to get involved in new activities and new challenges.'

'In order that people may be happy in their work, these three things are needed: They must be fit for it. They must not do too much of it. And they must have a sense of success in it.'
JOHN RUSKIN, British critic

Defining idea...

The interviewers are unlikely to go into the specifics of what went wrong with the team, unless you're going for an internal job. In the latter case you need to research carefully what's caused the demoralisation.

How did it go?

Q **When I suggested that bonuses play a part in team motivation I was asked, 'Doesn't that sound a bit like buying your way out of your duties as a leader?' What's the answer to that?**

A   *The best answer is to avoid being asked that question. Perhaps you overdid the bonuses bit at the expense of other types of reward. Make sure you've put enough emphasis on appreciation and involvement. If you do get that reaction, try, 'Good heavens, no! Money is only a part of motivation. You can't ignore it, but you can't rely on it to do the whole job.'*

Q **When I talked about running a planning process, the interviewer told me that, if given the job, I'd have a two-day away session to do our plan, facilitated by an outside resource. She was sceptical that I could do it without that sort of resource. Are you suggesting I should be able to do what a facilitator does?**

A   *Yes. You can always use the same process to review the plan during the year. You've got to be able to do this stuff, because events can occur that require a radical review of the plan at any time; events don't wait until the annual session comes along. However, if your boss offers a facilitator, take them up on it: you'll be able to give your full attention to the plan itself rather than to managing the event.*

50

How do you get things done?

Research shows that all successful managers are strong in two areas: general intelligence (helps you to figure things out) and conscientiousness (helps you to get things done). Here's a series of questions specifically about the latter.

They're going to try to pin down how hard and meticulously you work and how effective you are.

There's not a lot they can ask about your general intelligence. They'll look at your education and qualifications. They'll look at your analytical skills and judgement by asking questions about your experience and possibly give you a series of tests. That leaves us with conscientiousness.

JUST HOW EFFECTIVE ARE YOU?

'Tell me about a time when you had to work extremely hard to ensure that a project was completed.' This is fairly straightforward but there's one lurking snake. Be careful that your reply doesn't make it look as though you left things to the last minute or didn't have a proper work plan. Taking something over would be a good example, as would responding to an external event that changed things: 'I was managing the project to support the maintenance of a new product. The timescale we had planned for was fifteen months. Then a competitor brought out a similar product and the board decided to move more quickly with ours. We had to shave

Here's an idea for you... **Prepare at least two PERL project examples, big or small. You'll almost certainly get a question that will tee up these stories and they'll have the ingredients they're looking for: good business process and methodical implementation backed by talent, i.e. conscientiousness.**

three months off the original plan.' Lay it on thick if you can: 'And it was Christmas the month before the new completion date.'

Now show that you didn't just go flat out, you sat down and made a plan: 'I got the team together and we discussed the situation frankly and agreed we were going to go for it. We warned our families that we would be at work for a lot more time than usual and arranged for most of the team to take time off after the finish.'

Now explain how the team rose to it: 'The team were amazing. We were so close knit and cooperative that we completed the first pilot test on site before the launch. What did it was terrific communication, a plan that everyone bought into and then, well, long hard hours. Very rewarding at the end for all of us.'

Notice how the team gets given the credit all the time. So that's the template: something unexpected, a complete re-plan, thoughtfulness about the team and success.

'Tell me of a time when you had to cut through organisational barriers.' Don't make it look as though you hadn't expected the barrier. Use something unexpected again. Demonstrate what you did with your ability to get people in other departments to cooperate. But mention also some top-level support. They're not looking for someone who goes out on a limb without some sort of safety rope. Don't forget to spell out the benefit to the company of your breaking the rules.

The interviewers might ask a very straightforward question about this. See IDEA 21, *Do you enjoy hard work?*

Try another idea...

HAVING A LOT OF BALLS IN THE AIR

Conscientiousness includes juggling with priorities. 'Tell me about a time when you had to adjust your priorities in order to meet a new and urgent requirement.' Start in the same way by making sure that the change in priorities doesn't come across as a planning problem. If you've taken the initiative, that's good: 'Because sales had gone well, I realised that bringing out the top of the range before the mid-range would improve profitability.' Keep it action oriented. Yes, they want to hear there was a plan, but they also want to know what you did and how you got people to do their bit.

'Tell me about the biggest goal you had to achieve last year. What steps did you take to meet that goal?' PERL is useful here: Plan, Execute, Reflect and Learn. You made a plan, you implemented it with frequent pauses to evaluate what you were doing, and you learnt a lot as the team went through the project.

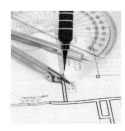

'The Way of our Master is none other than conscientiousness and altruism.'
CONFUCIUS

Defining idea...

217

How did it go?

Q **I found PERL interesting, but it doesn't work. We work quite well as a team. I have no problems getting people together to make a plan or to monitor how the plan is being executed. But when I tried to call a meeting to reflect on what we were doing almost everyone cried off because they were too busy doing things to move the project along – they were executing. How can you argue with them?**

A *You need a result here. Make a couple of one-to-one meetings happen, formally or informally. Talk about the project and ask the other person for suggestions as to how you could improve the processes you're going through. In our experience they'll all come up with something and that is the point of 'reflect'.*

Q **I left school when I was seventeen despite everyone saying I should stay on and go to university. I couldn't bear the fact that all my mates were earning money; so I got a job. I'm twenty-five now and trying to get a job in management. While I can make good arguments about my conscientiousness, will people suspect my intelligence and regard it as a barrier to my becoming a manager?**

A *We only said that education was one way by which employers will seek an indication of intelligence. The work you've done will probably compensate for your lack of qualifications, but there are, we're afraid, people out there who regard a lack of qualifications as a deal breaker for senior jobs. You'll probably succeed through your endeavours and results, but maybe you should think about a relevant qualification that you could do at the same time as a full-time job. Many employers support their people doing this, because it's in their interests too.*

51

How good are your time-management and presentation skills?

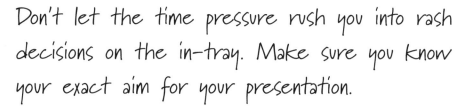

Two items that often come up in second interviews or assessment centres are in-tray exercises and presentations.

Don't let the time pressure rush you into rash decisions on the in-tray. Make sure you know your exact aim for your presentation.

They can simulate your in-tray very dramatically nowadays, with twenty emails in your inbox, your computer buzzing to signal an urgent message and a tray overflowing with paperwork.

BE SYSTEMATIC AND BE SEEN TO BE SYSTEMATIC

Don't act on the items as they come. Make sure you've read everything before you make any decisions. There could be a snake at the bottom of the pile. It's also likely that one item will have an impact on another. The most popular way of handling an in-tray exercise is, like all great techniques, very simple. Put the paperwork and emails into three categories – A, B, C – by assessing their urgency and impact. 'Urgent' is something that's got to be done or it'll be too late. 'Impact' measures

Here's an idea for you...

It's a good idea to announce at the start of a role-play presentation exactly what you want the group to decide at the end. The audience then knows where you're going to take them. Some people avoid this, since there's a risk that someone in the audience will tell you it won't be possible to achieve your aim; but logically it is better to know this at the start of the presentation than at the end. If you know what the audience's objections are, you may be able to use the presentation to overcome them.

how much an item affects the profit-and-loss account or other people.

A: Stuff that you think is urgent, that in real life you would do today – things you're going to deal with during the exercise. Matters to do with customers are most likely to occupy this category.

B: Stuff that's important but not as urgent as A. You'll get round to these today only if you finish with A. Tomorrow these matters could well go into A.

C: Material that may still be important. You need to know where it is, so that if something happens that changes its urgency or impact you can promote the item to A or B.

If during the exercise they interrupt you with phone calls, establish quickly who is calling and what their position is. You'll want to speak immediately to your boss, for example, since they may well change at least one of your priorities. When these interruptions occur, make sure that an observer can see you're applying the same systematic rules to each one, and putting those that don't need action now into C, even when someone on the phone says the matter's urgent.

PRESENTATION TIPS

If you're not a natural at presentations, go on training until you can at least survive. Ken knows one senior manager who made it to the top and remained a complete liability on his feet. When asked how he'd survived he replied, 'Ducking and weaving, old boy. I avoided presentations like the plague.'

The best tips for making effective presentations are the usual suspects: set tight objectives and talk exclusively in terms the audience will understand. The easiest way to set objectives for a presentation is to write down, 'At the end of this presentation the audience will:

- do something
- be able to do something
- have a certain attitude towards an event or plan.

This works well for an interview presentation and makes your preparation easier and quicker. In an interview, you will also have in mind the impression of you that you want to leave behind. For example: 'They'll see my drive and energy, my good listening skills and the fact that I work thoughtfully without making rash decisions.'

During your preparation, try to put yourself in the audience's shoes. This should help you to use only the language that they use and understand. Don't forget when you're planning your magnificent opening that you've also got to finish with a bang. (We've both found that 'Er, well, that's it' is a frequently used ending.) Allow time for questions and think through what the questions are likely to be, so you can

Other exercises in assessment centres are covered in IDEA 38, *Can we ask you to do a role-play and some group exercises?*

Try another idea...

'Unless one is a genius, it is best to aim at being intelligible.'
SIR ANTHONY HOPE HOSKINS, British novelist

Defining idea...

221

Defining
idea...

'**Presentations are about
them, the audience, rather
than you, the speaker.**'
RICHARD HUMPHREYS, British
venture capitalist

respond professionally. Lots of good
presentations founder at question time. Only
cover the main points on the visual aids, make
sure they have impact and don't just read
them out. They're aids for you to talk round.

How did
it go?

**Q   I tried to do the ABC analysis but it went wrong. A lot of the in-
tray was email. I tried to add the letters A, B or C on to the
messages, but got confused and in the end missed a really
important item. What should I have done?**

*A   Either print out the emails or put the topic and a reference to the email on
a piece of paper – or better a spreadsheet if you're quick at raising those.
You can then sort the emails as you do everything else.*

**Q   I was making a presentation to three people. Suddenly one of
them made a point and another one bluntly disagreed with her. In
no time they were at it hammer and tongs. I tried to break in, but
in the end just looked like a raw prawn as I tried to get my voice
heard. What were they doing?**

*A   This is almost certainly a set-up to see if they can rattle you. Stop trying to
present, look appealingly at the chairperson and, if they don't intervene,
try, 'We've obviously got a disagreement here. Can I suggest that we move
on and talk about that later on?'*

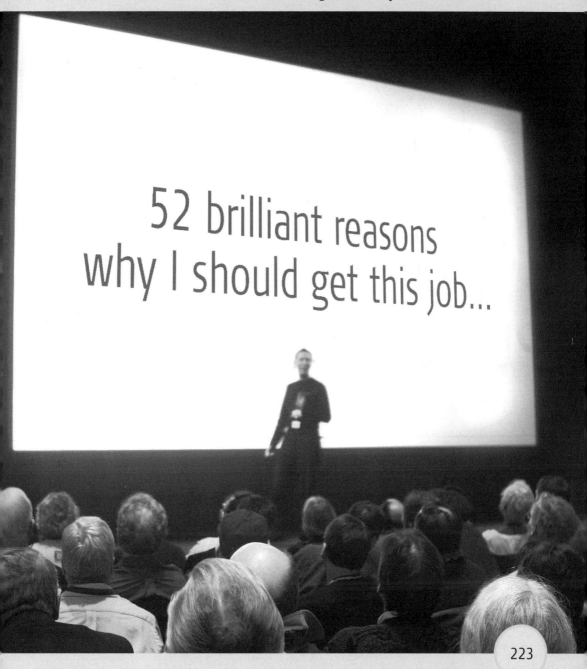

52

Is the gap between what you want and what we're offering significant enough to stop you taking the job?

The interviewer seems to have moved into negotiating mode. In answering this type of question remember that they're in a competitive position too – you could go and work for someone else.

Interviewing is not an exact science and interviewers aren't necessarily rocket scientists. They go on their emotions as much as anyone and when they've decided they want you they'll do all they can to get you.

Let's assume that this question is asked when they've pretty much made you an offer and you're talking terms and conditions. In this situation it's good technique to move the selling job from you to them. This is probably the strongest position you can be in to get the best deal out of them.

Here's an idea for you... **By using recruitment agencies, the internet and the personnel department you should be able to work out the salary range for the position you're applying for. Now work out why your experience and abilities mean that you deserve to be in the top 25% of the band. The top 25% is normally reserved for the real high-fliers in the organisation.**

WHAT'S IN IT FOR ME?

Interviewers take to people who have the confidence to make them do some selling too; so don't beat around the bush. It's never wrong to keep it simple: 'Why do you think that your company might be best for my career?' Keep in mind that it's you they want and, you never know, there may be more than one opportunity available. It's not infrequent for people to be offered a different job to the one they were interviewing for. So, if in these circumstances there is something about the job you don't quite like, not just the salary, talk about it now.

Perhaps the job description lacks something you like doing. 'I was rather hoping that there would be more contact with the product development people in this role. Who actually does the liaison work between research and development and the production department?' A question like this may well make them start to think of other ways they could organise things, or even talk about a different role for you. Don't burn your boats. For whatever reason, you may have to come back to the role as it is. But in our experience interviewees are more likely to err on the side of not pushing as hard as they might.

IT'S TERMS *AND* CONDITIONS YOU NEED TO DISCUSS

If you're disappointed by the starting salary, don't just accept their first bid if you think it's less than it should be. 'Well, that base salary is below my expectation. I don't want to reject it out of hand; but I'll need to think about it. Could I ask if you have any flexibility in this area?'

If you have got another offer then you can certainly use it as a lever. 'I have another offer that's 20% more than yours. If you could offer to halve that gap I would be delighted to join you.' If they will not move, you can try to make the first salary review much earlier than it might have been, particularly if you can tie it into a performance result. 'If I join at that salary and bring in five new customers in the first three months would you be prepared to review my salary at that point?'

They may convince you, probably erroneously, that company guidelines prevent them changing the salary that comes with the job. In this case, look at the rest of the package and see if there is anything else that could be improved: leave days, pension contributions, type of car or whatever. Just make sure you get as much out of them as you can at this advantageous point in the relationship.

IDEA 48, *What reservations would you have if we offered you the role?* looks at judging whether the job is the right one for you.

Try another idea...

> **'Let us never negotiate out of fear. But let us never fear to negotiate.'**
> ROBERT KENNEDY, US politician

Defining idea...

227

How did it go?

Q   **I nearly lost it because of you. The interview was going well and this exact situation arose. They wanted me to come for less than I thought I should get after researching the top-quartile salary. I held my ground and they suddenly went icy and said that they'd think about it. They then kept me on tenterhooks for nearly a week before offering me the job at the same salary. I took it, having suffered among the worst five days of my business life. What do you have to say for yourselves?**

A   *OK, sorry. Perhaps we should have said that you've got to keep the conversation friendly while the negotiation goes on. If you hit the salary question too hard you might have made them think that it was only the money you were after – never a good impression to leave. On the other hand, they may have out-negotiated you. Perhaps they let you sweat to get you on their terms. Bad luck. We'll never know for sure.*

Q   **I really meant to try to get a better deal than the one they were offering; but when the moment came I really wanted the job and I took it. It's hard to face the feeling that you're putting the job offer at risk by asking for more, don't you think?**

A   *Couldn't agree more, and in the end you've got the job you wanted and they're paying the salary they think is right. The next thing to do is work out when to ask for more money once you're in the job. The best time is when you have just done something that has really made a contribution. So don't wait for the annual appraisal; go for it at the first opportunity.*

The end...

Or is it a new beginning? We hope that the ideas in this book will have equipped you with the interview techniques that you need to get your dream job. You know you're the person they want, and now you understand the questions they're going to ask it should be no problem for you to convince them of that.

So why not let us know about it? Tell us how you got on. What did it for you – what helped you to breeze through the in tray task or out-psych the psychometric test? Maybe you've got some tips of your own you want to share (see the next page if so). And if you liked this book you may find we have even more brilliant ideas that could change other areas of your life for the better.

You'll find the Infinite Ideas crew waiting for you online at www.infideas.com.

Or if you prefer to write, then send your letters to:
Knockout interview answers
The Infinite Ideas Company Ltd
36 St Giles, Oxford OX1 3LD, United Kingdom

We want to know what you think, because we're all working on making our lives better too. Give us your feedback and you could win a copy of another *52 Brilliant Ideas* book of your choice. Or maybe get a crack at writing your own.

Good luck. Be brilliant.

Offer one

CASH IN YOUR IDEAS

We hope you enjoy this book. We hope it inspires, amuses, educates and entertains you. But we don't assume that you're a novice, or that this is the first book that you've bought on the subject. You've got ideas of your own. Maybe our authors have missed an idea that you use successfully. If so, why not send it to yourauthormissedatrick@infideas.com, and if we like it we'll post it on our bulletin board. Better still, if your idea makes it into print we'll send you four books of your choice or the cash equivalent. You'll be fully credited so that everyone knows you've had another Brilliant Idea.

Offer two

HOW COULD YOU REFUSE?

Amazing discounts on bulk quantities of Infinite Ideas books are available to corporations, professional associations and other organisations.

For details call us on:
+44 (0)1865 514888
fax: 44 (0)1865 514777
or e-mail: info@infideas.com

The questions...

Where it's at...